THE NEW INDONESIAN HOUSE

ROBERT POWELL

photographs by ALBERT LIM KS

TUTTLE Publishing

Tokyo | Rutland, Vermont | Singapore

Published by Tuttle Publishing, an imprint of Periplus
Editions (HK) Ltd

www.tuttlepublishing.com

Text © 2010 Robert Powell
Photographs © 2010 Albert Lim Koon Seng

ISBN 978-0-8048-4143-6

Distributed by:
North America, Latin America & Europe
Tuttle Publishing
364 Innovation Drive, North Clarendon, VT 05759-9436, USA
Tel: 1 (802) 773-8930; Fax: 1 (802) 773-6993
info@tuttlepublishing.com
www.tuttlepublishing.com

Asia Pacific
Berkeley Books Pte Ltd
61 Tai Seng Avenue, #02-12, Singapore 534167
Tel: (65) 6280-1330; Fax: (65) 6280-6290
inquiries@periplus.com.sg
www.periplus.com

Japan
Tuttle Publishing
Yaekari Building, 3rd Floor, 5-4-12 Osaki
Shinagawa-ku, Tokyo 141 0032
Tel: (81) 3 5437-0171; Fax: (81) 3 5437-0755
sales@tuttle.co.jp
www.tuttle.co.jp

Printed in Singapore

15 14 13 12 11
6 5 4 3 2 1

Front endpaper The sun rises over misty valleys below Dago
House No. 1 in Bandung (page 104).

Back endpaper Sunset over the K House (page 68).

Page 1 The high-ceilinged dining area of the Ampera House
(page 156) overlooks a secluded garden with a glittering blue
swimming pool.

Page 2 The transparent entrance lobby of the Ampera House
(page 156).

Pages 4–5 Beneath the curved roof form of the Kayu Aga
House (page 120), transparent "boxes" house the living area
and kitchen/dining area.

Pages 6–7 A steel mesh "veil" overlays the concrete-framed
Joelianto Residence (page 34).

Contents

The Ridwan Kamil House (page 58) has a façade constructed from 30,000 recycled Red Bull bottles.

the new indonesian house

The first decade of the twenty-first century saw a remarkable surge in the quality of residential architecture in Indonesia. The architects who are at the forefront of this phenomenon are the product of a "revolution" that occurred in the late 1980s when a group of undergraduates at the University of Indonesia came together to produce "Architrave," the internal journal put together by students from the department of architecture. Irianto Purnomo Hadi, Yori Antar, Sonny Sutanto, Achmad Noerzaman, Boy Bhirawa, Ranuwijaya and Syahrul Partawijaya upgraded what had previously been a basic publication of stenciled prints to a magazine featuring current architectural issues, and produced four editions that were circulated to other campuses.

Without realizing it, they put in motion a significant shift in Indonesian architecture, because the magazine paved the way for the formation, in 1989, of Arsitek Muda Indonesia (AMI) or Forum of Young Indonesian Architects, as students from other campuses eagerly followed up the topics. Irianto Purnomo Hadi now looks back on those days and reflects that "It was history in the making. It feels strange for we were just a bunch of unpretentious kids, but with a lot of energy, enthusiasm and ambition."[1]

Two decades have passed and members of AMI now form a nexus at the core of the profession in Indonesia. Most of the houses in this book are by members of the group who, in parallel with their contemporaries in Singapore, Malaysia, Thailand and the Philippines, have, to quote Philip Goad, "moved beyond the attractive formal signs of so-called regional architecture, to a re-thinking of the fundamental issues of space, material practice, tropicality, sustainability, urbanity and place—in essence a return to Ignasi de Sola Morale's 'ground zero' for architecture, a sort of phenomenological and existential base for the production of architecture...."[2]

INTRODUCTION

IN THE LAST TWO DECADES OF THE TWENTIETH CENTURY, ARCHITECTURAL DISCOURSE IN MANY ASIAN COUNTRIES THAT WERE COLONIZED BY EUROPEAN POWERS REVOLVED AROUND THE NOTIONS OF "IDENTITY"[3] AND "CRITICAL REGIONALISM."[4] IN 1985, DR SUHA ÖZKAN, AT THAT TIME DEPUTY SECRETARY-GENERAL OF THE AGA KHAN AWARD FOR ARCHITECTURE (AKAA), COMMISSIONED ME TO EDIT THE PROCEEDINGS OF A SEMINAR HELD IN KUALA LUMPUR ON THE SUBJECT OF "ARCHITECTURE AND IDENTITY." THIS SEMINAR, THE FIRST IN A SERIES TITLED "EXPLORING ARCHITECTURE IN ISLAMIC CULTURES," WAS ORGANIZED BY THE AKAA AND THE UNIVERSITI TEKNOLOGI MALAYSIA. ROBI SULARTO SASTROWARDOYO, THE FORMER HEAD OF THE ARCHITECTURE DEPARTMENT AT UDAYANA UNIVERSITY IN BALI AND A FOUNDING PARTNER OF ATELIER ENAM, DELIVERED ONE OF THE KEYNOTE PAPERS ON THE THEME OF ARCHITECTURAL IDENTITY IN INDONESIA, ESTABLISHED THROUGH ADHERENCE TO THE PANCASILA MAXIMS OF *BHINNEKA TUNGGAL IKA* OR "UNITY IN DIVERSITY."

The seminar was my introduction to the contemporary architecture of Southeast Asia and specifically to the architectural issues in the post-colonial Islamic world. When I subsequently edited the proceedings of two other AKAA seminars, the first held in Bangladesh in 1986 on "Regionalism in Architecture" and the second in Zanzibar in 1988 on "The Architecture of Housing," I encountered two other distinguished academics from Indonesia.[5] Professor Hasan Poerbo from Bandung University and Professor Johan Silus from the Surabaya Institute of Technology, together with Budi A. Sukada, then editor of the *Journal of Ikatan Arsitek Indonesia*, all spoke on the public housing programs in Indonesia, and thus my interest in the architecture of Indonesia was kindled.

Between 1993 and 2009 I returned to Indonesia on numerous occasions in the course of writing a series of eight books on contemporary architecture in Southeast Asia, including *The Asian House* (1993), *The Tropical Asian House* (1996), *The Urban Asian House* (1998) and *The New Asian House* (2001). The books were among the first to celebrate contemporary houses and included a romantic villa in Bogor by Jaya Ibrahim, an essay in deconstruction by Sardjono Sani, a quiet modern home by Tan Tjiang Ay, and other houses by the renowned artist Sunaryo, Ismeth Abidin, Solichin Gunawan and Ani Isdiati, Adhi Moersid of Atelier Enam, Muhammad Thamrin and Susiani Silalahi of Rekamatra, and Irianto Purnomo Hadi and Richard Dalrymple of PAI. The books also included "Bali-style" houses by Hendra Hadiprana and Faried Masdoeki of Grahacipta Hadiprana, and expatriates such as Michael White (Made Wijaya), Patrick Collins, Leonard Lueras and Rudolfo Giusti. It was on one of these visits that I encountered the work of the renowned Sri Lankan architect Geoffrey Bawa on the Batujimbah Estate at Sanur. Later, as consultant editor of *Space* magazine (Singapore) from 1999 to 2001, I published work by Andra Matin and Cheong Yew Kuan.

ARCHITECTURE IN INDONESIA AFTER INDEPENDENCE

TO UNDERSTAND THE RESIDENTIAL ARCHITECTURE OF INDONESIA AT THE END OF THE FIRST DECADE OF THE TWENTY-FIRST CENTURY, IT IS NECESSARY TO BEGIN WITH A BRIEF OVERVIEW OF THE SECOND HALF OF THE PRECEDING CENTURY AND EVENTS FOLLOWING INDEPENDENCE IN 1945.⁶ THE POLITICAL CLIMATE AT THE TIME CONTRIBUTED SIGNIFICANTLY TO THE ACCEPTANCE OF MODERN ARCHITECTURAL CONCEPTS. THE FIRST PRESIDENT OF THE NEW REPUBLIC, SUKARNO, HAD TRAINED AS A CIVIL ENGINEER AT THE TECHNISCHE HOGESCHOOL IN BANDUNG.⁷ HE HAD VERY CLEAR VIEWS ON ARCHI-TECTURE AND URBAN PLANNING, AND THEREFORE MODERNITY WAS ACCORDED A POWERFUL SYMBOLIC IMPORTANCE AS AN INDICATOR OF NATIONAL UNITY.

The first architectural school in Indonesia was established in October 1950 at the Institute of Technology in Bandung (ITB) and was modeled on the curriculum at Delft University of Technology in the Netherlands. By the early 1960s, works of the twentieth-century "masters," Frank Lloyd Wright, Walter Gropius and Le Corbusier, found their way into the curriculum, partly as a result of a twinning arrangement with the University of Kentucky in the USA, and students were strongly influenced by publications on modern architecture designed by Alvar Aalto in Scandinavia and Walter Gropius in Germany.⁸

Sukarno's vision of Indonesia as the fulcrum of a new world order culminated in the Bandung conference of non-aligned nations that brought together the leaders of Pakistan, Sri Lanka, India and Myanmar (or Burma as it was then known) in 1955. Sukarno, who portrayed himself as the first leader of the Non-Aligned Movement, hosted the conference.

Modern architecture took on huge political significance in Sukarno's "Guided Democracy," and in this respect there were parallels with other Southeast Asian countries. In the Philippines, during the presidency of Ferdinand Marcos (1965–86), architect Leandro Locsin designed a number of powerful modern symbols, such as the Theater of Performing Arts in the Cultural Center of the Philippines (1969). In neighboring Singapore, which became a republic in August 1965 following its secession from the Federation of Malaysia, modern archi-tecture, such as that produced by, for example, William Lim Siew Wai, Lim Cheong Keat and Chen Voon Fee of The Malayan Architects Co-Partnership in their design for the Singapore NTUC Conference Hall (1965), expressed the aspirations of the new republic.

Architect Friedrich Silaban, who was influenced by Le Corbusier, came closest to realizing Sukarno's nationalist ideals in architecture and urban design. Silaban's projects,

The Bea House (page 48) has a distinctive linear form.

mainly in Jakarta, including the Bank Indonesia building, which utilized a modern architectural language appropriated from European modernism. And in the 1960s, a group of young Indonesian students in the Netherlands came together under the banner of ATAP (literally interpreted as "roof"), to reject the idea that Indonesian architecture could be characterized through applying traditional forms. The group included architects Soejoedi, Han Awal, Bian Poen, Soewondo Bismo Soetedjo and his wife Wan Jin, and Mustafa Pamoentjak.

Sukarno's successor, Suharto, took over the reins of power in March 1967 and led a strong, central, military-dominated government for thirty years. At this time, the question of "identity" surfaced in architectural discourse. Under Suharto's "New Order" government, Indonesia pursued the *Pancasila* maxim of "Unity in Diversity." Unity was associated with the past and respect for cultural traditions. The revival of traditional cultures was linked to the public image of the New Order, and the establishment of Taman Mini Indonesia Indah (TMII) in 1975 became an expression of the ideology of Pancasila.[9] The implications of TMII were considerable in restraining the modern tendencies of the previous regime. Suharto, who was said not to have a strong affinity with modernism, played a part in promoting the use of ethnic architectural themes in public buildings. Traditional architecture was often used in an inflated form and became associated with "national" identity, whereas modern architecture became identified with "foreign" or "Western." A building with a rational modernist plan would often be topped with a traditional roof form—usually with decidedly unsatisfactory aesthetic results.

By the mid-1970s, the question of national architectural style and identity had become a controversial issue for Indonesian architects. The issue was discussed in academic institutions with great passion and the identity question had parallels in other Southeast Asian countries.

Architectural Identity was often seen as the resolution of a "paradox" expressed by the French philosopher Paul Ricour in his 1965 essay on "Universal Truths and National Cultures," in which he wrote, "In order to get on the road to modernisation, is it necessary to jettison the old cultural past? … On the one hand the nation has to root itself in the soil of its past, forge a national spirit and unfurl this spiritual and cultural revindication of the colonists personality. But in order to take part in modern civilisation, it is necessary at the same time to invest in scientific, technical and political rationality: something which often requires the pure and simple abandonment of a whole cultural past. There is the paradox; how to become modern and to return to your sources."[10]

And more to the point—what are the sources? Architecture in Indonesia has always been incredibly diverse, and the traditional vernacular architecture includes influences from numerous cultures, including Chinese (Buddhist and Christian), Indian (mainly Hindu) and Middle Eastern Islamic traditions, in addition to Dutch colonial and Indische architecture. In fact,

one might reasonably ask whether an "authentic" Indonesian architecture actually exists, even with reference to the country's vernacular work, which is highly diverse from an ethnic perspective. Contemporary architects in Indonesia were essentially faced with the same situation that existed in other Asian countries—how to modernize while maintaining a core of cultural identity.

The architecture of Y. B. Mangunwijaya, also known as Romo Mangun, stands out in this respect. According to his contemporary Han Awal, many Indonesian architects were deeply influenced by modern Western architects of the likes of Oscar Niemeyer and Le Corbusier. "But Romo Mangun was different," says Han. "After training at the Institute of Technology Bandung he continued his studies at the Rhineland-Westphalia Institute of Technology in Aachen, Germany, and Mangunwijaya should have been following the mainstream in architecture." But, according to Han, who helped Romo Mangun on the project, "Romo Mangun's buildings were always made with an eye to local tradition. For example, when he built a church in Cilincing, North Jakarta, Romo Mangun wanted it to be in the Betawi (traditional Jakarta) style with a slightly slanted roof. Nevertheless, its interior was modern with four pillars supporting vaulted ceilings as Romo had seen in the West."

In another building, the Said Naum Mosque, designed in 1977 by Atelier Enam, traditional Javanese idioms were skillfully reinterpreted to produce a modern regional architecture compatible with the best indigenous work. The project was the recipient of an Aga Khan Award for Architecture in 1986. But these and the work of the design team for Universitas Indonesia's Administrative Center Building were exceptions.

ARSITEK MUDA INDONESIA

IN 1989, A GROUP OF YOUNG ARCHITECTURAL GRADUATES WHO HAD A COMMON INTEREST IN BROADENING DISCUSSION ABOUT ARCHITECTURE AND URBAN DESIGN IN INDONESIA FORMED ARSITEK MUDA INDONESIA (AMI) OR FORUM OF YOUNG INDONESIAN ARCHITECTS. THE GROUP WAS MOTIVATED BY THE PERCEIVED LACK OF A FORUM FOR IDEAS AT THE TIME AND IT MOVED RESOLUTELY TO CREATE A SPACE FOR COMMUNICATION, EXPERIMENTATION, EXHIBITIONS, PUBLICATIONS AND ARCHITECTURAL EXPLORATION AMONG YOUNG PROFESSIONAL ARCHITECTS, ACADEMICS AND STUDENTS IN INDONESIA.

Focusing on building design, urban space and public art, the group has subsequently broadened its base to include cultural commentators, sociologists, artists and NGO activists with similar concerns about the condition of the built and natural environment in Indonesia. Its attempt to return to the public a role in urban design and planning was underlined by its involvement during the post-riot situation in Jakarta and Solo in 1998–2000.[11]

The seven founding members of the group were Irianto Purnomo Hadi, Yori Antar and Sonny Sutanto (all graduates of the University of Indonesia and Sutanto subsequently of UCLA, USA), Andra Matin (Parahyangan Catholic University Bandung) and Sardjono Sani (Parahyangan Catholic University and subsequently the University of Colorado at Denver, USA), and Ahmad D. Tardyana and Bambang Eryudhawan (both graduates of the Institute of Technology Bandung, and subsequently the University of New South Wales, Australia). They resolved to promote their views with exhibitions of their work.

The group grew rapidly from seven to fifteen by the time of their first exhibition with the inclusion of Jeffrey Budiman and Marco Kusumawijaya (Parahyangan Catholic University), Achmad Noerzaman, Boy Bhirawa and Dicky Hendrasto (University of Indonesia) and Gatot Surarjo and Ahmad Rida Soemardi (Institute of Technology Bandung). From the outset, the members were resolved to be supportive of each other and to engender a spirit of openness, sharing and cooperation. They also resolved not to attack each other but to encourage exploratory discussions about architecture and to create a critical dialogue—something they felt to be lacking. Members of the group are all now in their late forties.

The original core group gradually expanded to embrace the "next generation of AMI" (sometimes referred to as AMINext), among them Adi Purnomo (Gajah Mada University, Yogyakarta),

Ahmad Djuhara, Wendy J. Djuhara, Kusuma Agustianto, Tan Tik Lam, Denny Gondojatmiko, Zenin Adrian, Maria Rosantina and Gregorius Supie Yolodi (all Parahyangan Catholic University), Andy Pratama (University of Indonesia), Sukendro "Kendro" Sukendar Priyoso and Jeffry Sandy (both Trisakti University, Jakarta), Ridwan Kamil (University of California at Berkeley, USA), Budi Pradono (Duta Wacana Christian University, Yogyakarta), Antony Liu, Ferry Ridwan and Yanto Effendi (all Tarumanagara University, Jakarta), Willis Kusuma (Tarumanagara University and subsequently the University of California, USA) and Idris Samad (Art Center Pasadena). Members of the next generation are now in their late thirties or early forties.

An even younger generation of architects that includes Danny Wicaksono (University of Trisakti), who works alongside Adi Purnomo in mamostudio, Agit Mohd Sagitha, Wiyoga, Dicky Padmawijaya, Ginanjar Randhani and Mohammad Hikmat Subarkah (all graduates of Parahyangan Catholic University), have been enthusiastic in perpetuating the aims of the group. The youngest members wryly refer to themselves as IPAMI (the Union of Employees of AMI)

Houses designed by members of Arsitek Muda Indonesia (AMI) comprise the majority of the dwellings featured in this book. This was not my intention at the outset, but as the book took shape I was drawn to the conclusion that since its inception the group has been a catalyst for change, experimentation and indeed the advancement of architecture in Indonesia.

I first came into contact with the members of AMI in 1994/95 when I was researching my book *The Tropical Asian House*. I met Sardjono Sani who had just completed a seminal house for his own family intriguingly named "The Nobody House," and I was subsequently introduced to Yori Antar, Achmad Noerzman and Ahmad Rida (Tata) Soemardi. The group had just published a book of their work entitled *AMI Exploration 1990–1995* that recorded their first exhibition at the National Monument in celebration of Indonesia's fiftieth anniversary of independence. In the words of Sonny Sutanto, the book essentially contained "propaganda to move Indonesian architecture in a different direction," for "AMI was a romantic revolution that tended to be egalitarian, (it was) the underdog, (and) faced the walls of the establishment, (with) an obvious enemy (in) stagnant paternalism."[12]

Gunawan Tjahjono put it is similar terms. "In 1990, AMI emerged from growing disappointment (with) the stagnant Indonesian architecture ... with a passion to challenge the weariness found in architectural designs at the time.... AMI's presence was a breath of fresh air and a revelation to sleeping Indonesian architecture. Finally, a dynamic movement took responsibility for Indonesian architecture...."[13]

In early 1999, the group celebrated their tenth year with a joint exhibition of their work. Launched in the Netherlands, the exhibition was later displayed in the Dutch Embassy in Jakarta, from December 1999 to January 2000. The group

published a second book, *Works and Projects of Young Indonesian Architects 1997–2002*, sometimes referred to as "the Orange Book," which illustrated the body of work emerging from AMI members.

Almost a decade passed until, in 2009, while researching the current publication, I was reunited with several of the founding members and encountered the next generation (AMINext), including Adi Purnomo, Ahmad and Wendy Djuhara and Gregorius Supie Yoladi.

In October 2009, at the time of our meeting, Ahmad Djuhara was the chairman of IAI (Ikatan Arsitek Indonesia) Jakarta Chapter while Andra Matin chaired the IAI Awards Jury in 2008 and Adi Purnomo received the institute's Gold Medal in the same year. This would seem to indicate that the group, once at the fringe of the profession, now occupies the center ground. Some, indeed, might be regarded as "the establishment": Achmad Noerzaman is now CEO of the giant Arkonin Group, a huge conglomerate of design professionals, while Dicky Hendrasto and Budiman Hendropurnomo are directors of PT Duta Cermat Mandiri, the Indonesian arm of Denton Corker Marshall, an Australian practice with global connections. AMI was also the moving force behind the Jakarta Architecture Triennale that was in session in November 2009.

The formation of AMI has parallels with similar groups in neighboring countries that sought to encourage critical thinking about architecture against a background of societal change. In 1990, William Lim Siew Wai and a group of graduates of the Architectural Association (AA) School of Architecture in London formed AAAsia based in Singapore, and Dr Ken Yeang initiated a similar group in Malaysia under the title Asian Design Forum (ADF) in May 1990.

It is also noteworthy that in addition to the hard core of AMI members from the University of Indonesia, another significant group, including Andra Matin, Sardjono Sani, Ahmad Djuhara, Kusuma Agustianto, Jeffrey Budiman, Tan Tik Lam and Gregorius Supie Yolodi, are graduates of the architecture school at Parahyangan Catholic University in Bandung, the oldest private architectural school in Indonesia and one which has enjoyed a status equal to the public universities since it was established in 1960.

Dr Johannes Widodo, now Associate Professor of Architecture at the National University of Singapore, was close to events. From 1984 to 2000 he was first Lecturer and later Senior Lecturer at Parahyangan Catholic University in Bandung. From 1996 to 1998 he was Head of Architecture. He recalls, "During the period 1986–2000, students' publications were thriving, such as PILAR (critical magazine), and later KREA (creative design journal). Many students were also involved in extra-curricular groups, such as ARJAU (Arsitektur Hijau or Green Architecture) and BX (Bandung Experiments). ARJAU is an activity group which combines adventure and scientific expeditions to explore nature and to map uncharted settlements across the Indonesian archipelago, while BX is a critical group focusing on learning and design experimentation to challenge the established design practice and curriculum in Indonesia. Many students who were involved in these publications and organizations later emerged as leaders, including those who founded AMI. Architecture students at Parahyangan Catholic University enjoyed a lot of intellectual and political freedom through those activities and channels during the most oppressive period of Suharto's rule; some of them (not many) were involved in political activism against Suharto, especially at an intellectual level. It was also a period when the Internet and computers became more accessible to students in Indonesia and there was free Internet access to students of architecture. All of these factors have con-tributed in the formation and progression of AMI as a move-ment, not just as an ordinary organization."[14]

The membership of AMI also drew on graduates of Taru-managara University, the University of Trisakti in Jakarta, Gajah Mada University and Duta Wacana Christian University in Yogyakarta, and the Institute of Technology Bandung.

The formation of AMI could be linked to societal and cultural shifts in the late 1980s. Yori Antar was the facilitator of the group, which gradually grew as its aims were passed on by word of mouth and Fax messages. Their primary concerns were the moribund state of the profession, which was dominated by large practices, and dissatisfaction with their professional institute that seemed to have little interest in

"good design." They agreed to mount an exhibition of their work—most of it conceptual, some of it small built works.

Irianto Purnomo Hadi, the first president of the group (in fact, the only president since they quickly agreed to drop the grandiose title) explains that "During the Suharto Regime it was generally the case that you had to say what the government wanted to hear. We simply 'agreed to disagree,' which in itself was a statement of rebellion."[15] It is evident that some senior members of the profession regarded the vocal group, who met every Wednesday evening in their first year of existence, with suspicion. Their habit of all wearing black was even seen as provocative and "elitist."[16]

The Asian financial crisis at the end of the 1990s had far-reaching consequences on the Indonesian economy and on society. With the collapse in the value of the Indonesian currency, foreign investment shrank, and there was wide-spread unemployment accompanied by food shortages and price rises. Increasingly, prominent political opponents spoke out against Suharto's presidency, and university students organized nationwide demonstrations. Abdurrahman Wahid, Chairman of Nahdulatul Ulama (NU), mobilized people behind the "Reformasi" movement. The shooting of four Trisakti University student demonstrators in Jakarta on May 12, 1998 triggered rioting across the city and in other cities such as Medan and Surakarta. Young architects, too, were moved to protest, and as Gregorius Supie Yolodi, a member of Arsitek Muda Indonesia, recalls, "1998 was a time of rebellion" against the status quo.[17] Following public outrage at the events, a student occupation of the parliament building, street pro-tests across the country, and the desertion of key political allies, on May 21, 1998 Suharto announced his resignation.

The immediate consequences of the 1998 riots on archi-tecture have been discussed most pertinently by Associate Professor Abidin Kusno in his incisive paper, "Back to the City: A Note on Urban Architecture in the New Indonesia." He states that "We do not know exactly the significance of the May riots in altering the subjectivities of Indonesian architects, but soon after the event, some architects pledged to make architec-ture sensitive to local cultures so that it would be accepted by society.…"

"There was," he wrote," a sense that the sharp line between the haves and the have-nots would have to be altered through architectural design and that one criteria for a good house is a house that unites with its surroundings. However that sentence is understood, it shows a change of consciousness if not architectural strategy in the post-Suharto era."[18]

From 1989 onwards, Arsitek Muda Indonesia engaged in discussions and exhibitions. Gradually, upper middle-class patrons accepted their works, which placed emphasis on visual appearance and design individuality. Sardjono Sani's family house in Pondok Indah, Andra Matin's Gedung Dua Delapan and Ahmad Djuhara's Steel House became icons for a new generation of architects. The Sixth IAI Award cycle in 1999 underlined this new direction in the discourse on

Indonesian architecture. The institute, alert to the shifting ground, stated that the criteria for winning an award was that architecture must "raise human dignity, be responsible to the social environment, and be sensitive towards the social context within which the building is embedded."

In writing at length on the emergence and effect of Arsitek Muda Indonesia, I am aware that this paints an incomplete picture since their activity has been largely confined to Jakarta and Bandung whereas, in reality, Indonesia is a vast archipelago. Eko Agus Prawoto, who practices and teaches in Yogyakarta, points out that "There is a different sensibility in Yogyakarta to that in Jakarta. Almost 75 percent of the wealth of the country passes through the capital and clearly that has an effect on architecture. In Yogyakarta, architects are required to 'do more with less.'"[19]

A HOUSE IN THE TROPICS

EKO PRAWOTO'S OWN ARCHITECTURE IS REMARKABLY SIMILAR TO THE ATTRIBUTES OF A DWELLING IN THE TROPICS SUMMARIZED IN MY 1996 THE TROPICAL ASIAN HOUSE. THE FIRST THREE CRITERIA WERE ARTICULATED IN A DISCUSSION WITH GEOFFREY BAWA WHILE WE DINED ON THE TERRACE OF HIS HOME AT LUNUGANGA IN SRI LANKA.[20] BAWA MAINTAINED THAT A HOUSE IN THE TROPICS IS ABOUT LIVING IN CLOSE PROXIMITY TO THE NATURAL WORLD, AND THEREFORE ANY SUBSTANTIAL TREES ON THE SITE SHOULD NOT BE DESTROYED. A HOUSE IN THE TROPICS, HE ASSERTED, SHOULD BE DESIGNED WITH THE MINIMAL USE OF GLASS. OTHER ATTRIBUTES INCLUDE THE USE OF GARDENS AND NON-REFLECTIVE SURFACES TO REDUCE RADIATED HEAT, WIDE OVERHANGING EAVES TO PROVIDE SHADE, THE OMISSION OF GUTTERS, THE USE OF IN-BETWEEN SPACES IN THE FORM OF VERANDAS, TERRACES AND SHADED BALCONIES, TALL ROOMS TO CREATE THERMAL AIR MASS AND PROVIDE THERMAL INSULATION, PERMEABLE WALLS FACING PREVAILING WINDS TO GIVE NATURAL VENTILATION, AND PLANS THAT ARE ONE ROOM DEEP WITH OPENINGS ON OPPOSITE SIDES CAPABLE OF BEING ADJUSTED TO PROMOTE NATURAL VENTILATION BY THE "VENTURI" EFFECT.

These criteria are still relevant in Indonesian architecture today but the urban house cannot be so pure. To this list must be added another imperative, namely duality between the public side of a house and the private side. This is linked to a perception of security, with the public side being "closed" and the private side "open."

The challenge facing architects in Jakarta and other cities in Indonesia is to design houses that permit their clients to live a relaxed open lifestyle with verandas, terraces and courtyard spaces while simultaneously solving issues of security. Living in a conurbation necessitates a variety of responses to the perceived threat of intruders, including high perimeter walls and electronic surveillance devices. A house in the city invariably includes some means of isolating and securing the family sleeping quarters at night.

The houses shown here embody a hierarchy of privacy with a public façade that seeks not to attract undue attention or to make an extravagant display of wealth, and interior spaces that embrace and shelter their occupants while opening out to courtyards and terraces. The houses provide a haven of calm and a "refuge" from the frantic pace of life in the city and seek to modify the effects of air pollution, noise and increasingly high temperatures that inevitably necessitate air-conditioning in some parts of a house.

THE EMERGENCE OF AN URBAN MIDDLE CLASS

THE EMERGENCE OF ARSITEK MUDA INDONESIA AND OTHER GROUPS SUCH AS FORUM ARSITEK MEDAN (FAM), BOMBARS IN MANADO, SAMM (SPIRIT ARSITEK MUDA MALANG) IN EAST JAVA AND DESAINER MUDA SURABAYA (DE MAYA), ALSO IN EAST JAVA, HAS BEEN PARALLELED BY THE GROWTH OF AN URBAN MIDDLE CLASS IN INDONESIA. THIS EXPANDING MIDDLE CLASS HAS, IN SOME CASES, STUDIED OVERSEAS AND TRAVELED WIDELY, IN THE PROCESS BECOMING CONVERSANT WITH ARCHITECTURE AND INTERIOR DESIGN ELSEWHERE. IT IS RELEVANT TO MENTION THE PHENOMENA AT THIS POINT FOR IT HAD AN EFFECT ON THE ARCHITECTURAL MODELS THAT FOUND FAVOR FROM 1989 ONWARD.[21]

In the early 1990s, as a result of a spate of books and magazines on architecture in the region, Indonesia's middle classes began to appreciate the country's own architects.[22] Home owners realized that Indonesian architects were capable of constructing houses that were sophisticated in design. Simultaneously, the growth of the Internet in the last decade of the twentieth century enabled images to be transferred across borders with phenomenal speed and brought awareness of design in other parts of Asia.

The New Indonesian House gives insights into the aspirations of the rapidly growing upper middle and upper classes in Indonesia, who operate in a dynamic and plural culture.

THE BALI EFFECT

THE POPULAR IMAGE OF TROPICAL ARCHITECTURE IN INDONESIA HAS LONG BEEN AND STILL IS LARGELY DRIVEN BY ORIENTALIST NOTIONS OF SOUTHEAST ASIA AS AN EXOTIC DESTINATION, AND BY CURRENT TOURIST ASPIRATIONS FOR A NON-WESTERN LIVING EXPERIENCE.[23]

The published residential architecture of Bali is dominated by the creations of numerous foreign architects who have taken up residence on the fabled island. Bali is a "different world," offering a sybaritic lifestyle that is quite divorced from Java and Sumatra. The question inevitably arises whether the production of resort-style dwellings is in any sense Indonesian. The houses there often appropriate traditional vernacular forms and materials for Western expatriate lifestyles.

I have published several of these exotic houses in earlier books, and indeed I have had the pleasure of vacationing in some of them. The lifestyles of the inhabitants are manifestly divorced from and, in most cases, in total contrast to the lives of the local people. Nevertheless, the design of houses for expatriates has had a profound effect on how the Indonesian house is perceived by non-Indonesians.

This new book contains examples of this genre but most are designed by Indonesian architects, including the Tukad Balian House, which is owned by an American landscape architect and his Indonesian wife and designed by Antony Liu and Ferry Ridwan; the Kayu Aga House, owned by an Italian businessman and designed by Balinese architect Yoka Sara; Villa Ombak Luwung, owned by a banker based in Singapore and designed by another Balinese architect, Popo Danes, and the Villa Kalyani, owned by a French banker based in Singapore and designed by Balinese architect Sekar Warni. Another of the houses, the Joelianto Residence, is owned by a Jakarta entrepreneur and is designed by Andra Matin, while Villa Dewi Sri is designed by an expatriate German architect, Walter Wagner. A house in the resort village of Alila Soori, owned by a Singaporean architect and his Indo-nesian partner, is designed by Chan Soo Khian of SCDA.

SOCIAL ISSUES

SOCIAL HOUSING IS A SUBJECT THAT FINDS ITS WAY INTO MOST CONVERSATIONS WITH YOUNG INDONESIAN ARCHI-TECTS. AHMAD DJUHARA BELIEVES STRONGLY THAT THIS IS A ROLE MORE ARCHITECTS SHOULD ENGAGE IN. IT IS ALSO A SUBJECT BROUGHT UP IN CONVERSATION WITH ECO AGUS PRAWOTO. IT IS EVIDENT THAT MANY ARCHI-TECTS, WHILE PRODUCING ENVIABLE DWELLINGS FOR THEIR AFFLUENT CLIENTS, WOULD WELCOME THE OPPOR-TUNITY TO BRING SOME OF THEIR EXPERTISE TO MASS HOUSING AND HOUSING FOR THE POOR.

In the past, there were architects in Indonesia who gave attention to these issues. Romo Mangun's desire to create dwellings for the poor was indisputable. During his time, there were a few other such architects who worked in this sphere. In Surabaya, there was Johan Silas. This professor, who helped establish the Technical and Architectural Department at the November 10 Institute of Technology in Surabaya, was one of the architects who helped create the Kampung Improvement Program (KIP). In Bandung, the late Hasan Poerbo, a professor in the Technology and Architecture Department at ITB, was also known as a "people's architecture" proponent and was

A "green roof" above the living area of Villa Dewi Sri (page 166) replaces vegetation lost by the very act of construction.

always concerned with the human aspect of each building. Aspects of "people's architecture" can also be seen in the works of Professor Eko Budihardjo, Rector of Diponegoro University in Semarang. Running through his writings is his belief that society is capable of building better, more cost-effective and simpler houses.

The gap between rich and poor is evident in Jakarta. The children of the wealthy are educated in universities overseas—in the USA, Singapore and the Netherlands, for instance—but it is common to encounter the children of the poor who walk barefoot and live under road viaducts and in squalid shacks alongside festering canals.

The Indian architect Charles Correa once famously said in the context of Mumbai that "The rich need the poor and the poor need the rich." This is not to suggest that class divisions should be perpetuated but it is evident that all the houses in this book could not function without maids, cooks, drivers and gardeners. It is an important consideration in the design of custom-designed dwellings.

There are "invisible walls" in dwellings that define the areas where domestic staff may be at certain times of the day. These flexible boundaries shift: when the maid is cleaning the house, she may have access to all parts of the house; when guests arrive, she fades into the background; when a child needs attention, she appears as if by magic; when the family is away, she has the run of the whole house, and when the family retires at night, she slips away to a small bedroom often little more than a boxroom. This is "maidspace" and can equally be applied to the situation of the ubiquitous driver. The extent to which architects and clients incorporate well-lit, well-ventilated habitable maidspace is a reflection of a country's maturity as a caring society.

INFLUENCES ON RECENT RESIDENTIAL ARCHITECTURE

OF THE TWENTY-SEVEN HOUSES FEATURED IN THIS BOOK, FOURTEEN ARE LOCATED IN JAKARTA, FIVE IN BANDUNG, ONE IN YOGYAKARTA AND SEVEN IN BALI. THE HOUSES REPRESENT THE WORK OF SOME NINETEEN INDONESIAN PRACTICES AND TWO SINGAPORE-BASED PRACTITIONERS, WITH WALTER WAGNER BEING THE SOLE EXPATRIATE ARCHITECT INCLUDED. SOME OF THE INDONESIAN ARCHITECTS PURSUED THEIR GRADUATE ARCHITECTURAL EDUCATION OVERSEAS AT DELFT UNIVERSITY OR THE BERLAGE INSTITUTE IN THE NETHERLANDS. OTHERS TOOK A ROUTE THAT LED THEM TO GRADUATE SCHOOLS AT THE UNIVERSITY OF COLORADO, THE UNIVERSITY OF FLORIDA AT GAINS-VILLE, THE UNIVERSITY OF CALIFORNIA LOS ANGELES AND THE UNIVERSITY OF CALIFORNIA BERKELEY IN THE USA, BUT A LARGE MAJORITY COMPLETED THEIR ARCHITECTURAL TRAINING IN INDONESIA.

The early masters of the modern movement have been a significant influence on the current generation of architects. Many young Indonesian architects refer to the seminal projects of Le Corbusier, Oscar Niemeyer, Mies van der Rohe, Alvar Aalto, Louis Kahn and Frank Lloyd Wright, and they are frequently mentioned as formative influences. The Japanese masters Tadao Ando and Kengo Kuma are evidently even more important influences, while nearer home Mangunwijaya and Tjiang Tan Ay have influenced several young architects.

Whereas the early meetings of AMI were summoned by hand-drawn missives sent via Fax by Yori Antar from the office of Han Awal, or by word of mouth, the youngest generation communicate by digital means and their circle has widened to include Indonesians studying overseas in Japan, Singapore and the USA. Between 2008 and 2010, sixteen issues of an E-Magazine entitled *Jong Arsitek* were published, and Danny Wicaksono believes that Indonesian architecture in the future will inevitably reflect global influences.

A JOURNEY WITHOUT MAPS

WRITING A BOOK ON RESIDENTIAL ARCHITECTURE IS A "JOURNEY WITHOUT MAPS." AT THE OUTSET, I HAD A VAGUE IDEA OF THE DESTINATION. BUT THE JOURNEY HAS BEEN ENRICHED BY EXPERIENCES BOTH PHYSICAL AND METAPHYSICAL. THERE HAVE BEEN UNEXPECTED ENCOUNTERS ALONG THE WAY; FRUSTRATING DETOURS AND THEN—NEW DISCOVERIES. AT TIMES, PROGRESS HAS BEEN HALTED BY UNCERTAINTY BUT OFTEN A CHANCE ENCOUNTER HAS GIVEN THE PROCESS NEW MOMENTUM.

For an architect, the design of a custom-made family dwelling is a demanding yet ultimately immensely rewarding commission. A designer rarely has such a close relationship with the end user. The most successful houses arise out of a strong empathy between the client and the designer. This compatibility is of critical importance because a house is ultimately "a social portrait of its owner."

The houses in this book illustrate exemplary residential architecture in Indonesia at the end of the first decade of the twenty-first century and demonstrate remarkable advances in design exploration in the country.[24] Architects are producing work with a level of refinement, sophistication and environmental awareness that is comparable with the best in the world. There are changing cultural responses and greater awareness of social and environmental issues—and this is resulting in new and frequently unconventional dwellings in the Indonesian context. We are witnessing the emergence of design genius in Indonesia that has been germinating since 1989. Nurtured by the intellectual debate within the architectural community and by increasingly knowledgeable patronage, it is blooming in a stunning variety of exhilarating architectural expressions.

1   Irianto Purnomo Hadi in correspondence with the author, March 12, 2010.

2   Philip Goad, *New Directions in Tropical Architecture*, Singapore: Periplus Editions, 2005, pp. 17–18.

3   Robert Powell (ed.), *Architecture and Identity: Exploring Architecture in Islamic Cultures 1*, Singapore: Concept Media for The Aga Khan Award for Architecture, 1983.

4   Robert Powell (ed.), *Regionalism in Architecture: Exploring Architecture in Islamic Cultures 2*, Singapore: Concept Media for The Aga Khan Award for Architecture, 1987.

5   Robert Powell (ed.), *The Architecture of Housing: Exploring Architecture in Islamic Cultures 4*, Geneva: The Aga Khan Award for Architecture, 1990.

6   Peter J. M. Nas and Martien de Vletter (eds), *The Past in the Present: Architecture in Indonesia*, Rotterdam: NAi Publishers, 2007.

7   In 2002, the IAI (Ikatan Arsitek Indonesia) honored Ir. Sukarno, the first President of Indonesia, "for his concern towards architectural discourse in Indonesia."

8   Tan Tjiang Ay in conversation with the author, February 10, 2010. Tan commenced his architecture studies at the ITB in 1958. Romo Mangun studied at the ITB in 1959 before embarking on architectural studies at the Rhineland-Westphalia Institute of Technology in Aachen, Germany.

9   Taman Mini Indonesia was a collection of the indigenous buildings of the twenty-six provinces of Indonesia assembled on a 100-hectare site in 1975.

10 Paul Ricoeur, "Universal Civilisations and National Cultures," in Charles A. Kelbley (trans.), *History and Truth*, Evanston: Northwestern University Press, 1965, pp. 271–84.

11 See Imelda Akmal, "The Architecture of 'Balinisation': An Investigation of Cultural Tourism Development in Bali," CSEAS Seminar Programme, Monash University, Melbourne, 2002.

12 Sonny Sutanto, "AMI 2002," in Imelda Akmal, Wendy Djuhara and P. Indrijati (ed.), *Karya-karya Arsitek Muda Indonesia/Works and Projects of Young Indonesian Architects 1997–2002*, Jakarta: Gramedia Pustaka Utama, 2002, p. 21.

13 Gunawan Tjahjono, "Young Indonesian Architects: The Exploration 1990–1995," in Imelda Akmal, Wendy Djuhara and P. Indrijati (ed.), *Karya-karya Arsitek Muda Indonesia/Works and Projects of Young Indonesian Architects 1997–2002*, Jakarta: Gramedia Pustaka Utama, 2002, p. 27.

14 Johannes Widodo in correspondence with the author, January 2, 2010.

15 Irianto Purnomo Hadi in conversation with the author, February 12, 2010.

16 Tan Tjiang Ay in conversation with the author, February 10, 2010.

17 Gregorius Supie Yolodi in conversation with the author, October 2009.

18 Kusno, Abidin, "'Back to the City': Urban Architecture in the New Indonesia," in *The Appearances of Memory: Mnemonic Practices of Architecture and Urban Form in Indonesia*, Durham: Duke University Press, 2010, pp. 71–97.

19 Eko Agus Prawoto in conversation with the author, February 11, 2010.

20 Geoffrey Bawa in conversation with the author, November 1994.

21 Amanda Achmadi, "Indonesia: The Emergence of a New Architectural Consciousness of the Urban Middle Class," in Geoffrey London (ed.), *Houses for the 21st Century*, Singapore: Periplus Editions, 2004, pp. 28–35. See also Amanda Achmadi, "The Quest for a New Tropical Architecture," in Amir Sidharta (ed.), *25 Tropical Houses in Indonesia*, Singapore: Periplus Editions, 2006, pp. 16–17.

22 See Robert Powell, *The Asian House* (1993), *The Tropical Asian House* (1996), *The Urban Asian House* (1998) and *The New Asian House* (2001).

23 Achmadi, "The Quest for a New Tropical Architecture," p. 8.

24 Inevitably, this book is a "snapshot" taken at a specific time (March 2010) and as such there are omissions. The intention was to include houses by architects Sardjono Sani, Dicky Hendrasto, Jeffrey Budiman, Baskoro Tedja and Irianto Purnomo Hadi. Time constraints and publishing deadlines meant that houses designed by these architects missed the cut.

radius muntu house

JAKARTA

ARCHITECT: TAN TJIANG AY

Tan Tjiang Ay is an Indonesian master architect who, in more than forty years in practice, has sustained a steady output of deceptively simple and elegant houses. His designs are unwaveringly modern but guided by an instinctive response to climate and locality. Most of his plans are one room deep and have wide overhanging eaves to provide natural ventilation and shade. He will always attempt to retain mature trees on the site and to provide "in-between" spaces at the periphery of the house to insure that there are places to sit that are at the interface between the interior and exterior.

It is these simple rules that have been applied to the design of the Radius Muntu House, a dwelling located in the heart of the city of Jakarta in an area surrounded by high-rise towers. Encountering a large and beautiful tree on the site persuaded Tan to split the accommodation and make a simple functional separation into daytime and night time areas and to place the living space, dining room, library and study in one pavilion and all the family sleeping accommodation in a separate block, together with a small outdoor gym and a hot tub. The obvious result is that in the event of heavy rainfall family members have to resort to using umbrellas to access the private rooms, but the owners accept this and indeed laugh off the suggestion that it is inconvenient, noting that it keeps their private life and that of their children separate from their public life. Preserving the tree was important for them as well.

The *pièce de résistance* of the house is without doubt the double-height open-sided living room that is essentially an outdoor living space in the city—a bold decision that works to perfection. This special space is attractive by day and stunningly so by night as the sun sets at the western end of the garden. The wide eaves obliterate views of the high-rise towers that encircle the site and prevent family activities from being seen. The dining room can be isolated from the living area if the heat or humidity becomes excessive. The

contrast and tension between the resort-style house and the towering city blocks that are visible from the garden are both daunting and yet exhilarating. As night descends, the city skyline becomes a fantastic sparkling backcloth.

The third component in the house plan is the arrival courtyard and a garage that is linked to the maid's quarters and a rooftop drying yard. The garage doors are elegantly detailed in perforated metal, and a rainwater downpipe is given some prominence, being oversized and painted in scarlet red.

Tan has gained a deserved reputation for designing beautiful and functional houses and his work is admired and emulated by a younger generation. His son, Tan Tik Lam, is also an architect and is continuing the family tradition of designing with understated elegance.

Pages 18–19 A courtyard separates the living and sleeping spaces.

Opposite A soaring double-height open-sided living room is the focus of the house.

Top The house is a haven of calm in the metropolis.

Above A small gymnasium is located on the veranda adjoining the master bedroom.

Above The private bedroom block is separated from the more public living/dining areas by a garden court.

Right Ground floor plan.

Key
1   Forecourt
2   Entrance gate
3   Garage
4   Living room
5   Dining room
6   Kitchen
7   Terrace
8   Powder room
9   Master bedroom
10 Dressing room
11 Bathroom
12 Hot tub

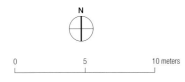

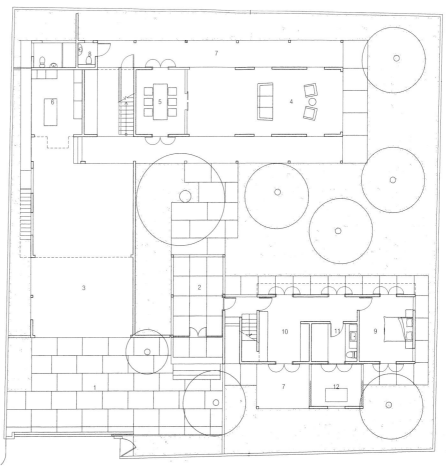

Right Entrance detail.

Far right The house is located in an inner city area and is surrounded by high-rise towers and communications masts.

Below The entrance court and garage present an intriguing façade to the public domain.

hudyana house

JAKARTA
ARCHITECT: RENÉ TAN
RT+Q ARCHITECTS

The Hudyana House is located on a rectangular corner site measuring 27 m x 29 m, with high walls on two sides and generous setbacks, in this case 8 m and 10 m, on the other two sides so that the footprint of the house is restricted to a 19 m x 19 m square in one corner. This is a typical urban site in Jakarta, and although an internal courtyard seems almost to be mandatory, it is remarkable how many variations can be achieved within the typology that makes each house unique and personal to the owner. A typical response is to create a U-shaped plan, with the principal rooms looking inward to a courtyard. Another common device is the insertion of perimeter lightwells to permit daylight to enter internal spaces and to assist in natural ventilation by the Venturi system.

In this instance, the architect, René Tan, and his colleague Jonathan Quek placed the courtyard on the outer edge of the dwelling facing the setback. It becomes a deep light-filled incision in the square form, permitting daylight to enter the principal rooms and borrowed light to filter into others. Tan also places a swimming pool in the perimeter setback space, insuring that maximum use is made of the whole site. The effect is that the house appears to be quite fragmented; indeed, the typology can even be read as an L-shaped plan embracing a square pavilion. Consequently, the dwelling is more transparent than most town houses and appears to be more spacious. The architect's stated intention was "to design a Platonic form amidst the diverse architectural languages of this upmarket area of Jakarta."[1]

The house is entered in the northwest corner (a feature of this urban typology is that the entrance is almost always at a corner). A guardhouse is located at the entrance, and the drive bifurcates, with a steep ramp down to the right to a basement garage and to the left to the entrance portico. The portico projects from a substantial stone wall pierced by the entrance lobby and a low horizontal window to the living room. The wall conveys a sense of security. Hovering above the stone base, like a fortress tower, is the master bedroom suite and a rooftop terrace, a superbly detailed steel and glass box clad in horizontal timber louvers to reduce insolation and to afford privacy.

Upon entering the house, a short covered veranda along the side of an open-to-sky courtyard leads to a lobby. To the left, behind a glazed wall, is the living room and to the right, slightly elevated, is a dry kitchen and breakfast bar—also with a glazed wall—resembling a stage. Visual connectivity is evident. The courtyard is also overlooked by the dining room with adjacent kitchen. A "junior master suite" comprising a bedroom and bathroom, both overlooking the swimming pool, completes the accommodation on the ground floor. The spatial choreography is exemplary and RT+Q succeeds in creating a myriad of spatial experiences.

Ascending to the first story, there is further evidence of the architect's skill at choreography, with a delightful series of spatial events. At the heart of the first-floor plan is the family room, surrounded by a guest suite, a child's bedroom, a prayer room and the master bedroom suite. In addition to the staircase, all three floors of the house are accessible by an elevator. At the very top of the house is an attic study and a roof terrace surrounded by a timber louvered opening screen wall and shaded by a canvas awning that is a delightful space for entertaining in the evening.

The Hudyana House is one of RT&Q's most mature works to date. René Tan goes from strength to strength, with a visible mastery of the genre. Backed by his hugely experienced partner, Jonathan Quek, his design skills are now sought by clients throughout Southeast Asia.

[1] E-mail correspondence with René Tan, February 23, 2010.

Pages 24–5 A massive stone wall and a fortress-like tower signal the entrance to the house.

Opposite View from the entrance court to the living room.

Above A shaded veranda skirts the entrance court and leads to the inner lobby.

Above The living room overlooks
a vibrant blue swimming pool.

Left All the principal rooms have
views into the courtyard.

Right An entrancing visitors' toilet,
with views out to the pool.

Opposite The breakfast room on the left is slightly elevated above the entrance court.

Left First floor plan.

Below In the evening, the roof-top terrace becomes a cool and breezy refuge.

Key
8   Bedroom
9   Bathroom
14 Family room
15 Master bedroom
16 Master bathroom
17 Wardrobe
18 Guest bedroom
19 Prayer room
20 Deck
22 Elevator

0   5   10 meters

Key
1   Car porch
2   Entrance
4   Dining room
12   Reflective pool
14   Family room
21   Study
24   Water feature
25   Function room

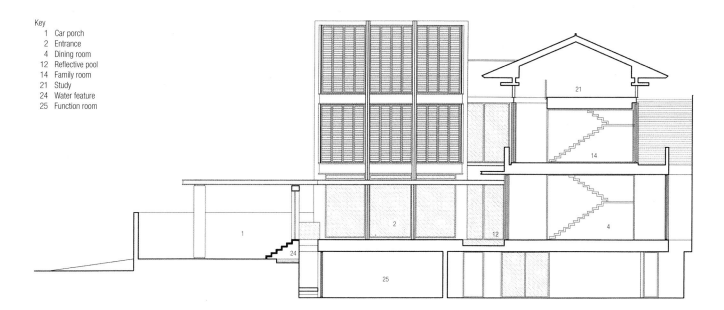

Left Section drawing.

Below left Hovering above the pool is the master bedroom suite and roof terrace clad in horizontal timber louvers.

Right The master bathroom.

Far right The processional route to the entrance.

Below The pool deck and azure pool viewed from the rooftop terrace.

joelianto
residence

SEMINYAK, BALI

ARCHITECT: ANDRA MATIN

ANDRAMATIN

Isandra (Andra) Matin Ahmad was born in Bandung in 1962 and graduated from the Parahyangan Catholic University, Bandung, in 1989 whereupon he took up a post with Grahacipta Hadiprana, initially as design architect on the Bali Intercontinental Resort at Jimbaran. He stayed with the practice until 1998, designing numerous projects, until he resigned to set up his own practice. Matin was one of the founding members of Arsitek Muda Indonesia (AMI) and today is considered to be one of the leading architects of his generation, producing highly innovative buildings.

The Joelianto House was designed for a Jakarta-based communications engineer and entrepreneur. The dwelling consists of two elements: a two-story rectangular pavilion containing private bed-rooms and bathrooms above an open-sided ground floor housing the living/entertainment area, dining area and open-plan kitchen; and a master bedroom suite with an attached outdoor bathroom in a smaller single-story pavilion. The larger of the two pavilions is conceptually a glass box within a louvered box. The two pavilions are arranged in an L-shaped configuration embracing a swimming pool and a water garden set inside a typical rectangular Balinese compound surrounded by a high wall. The owner, Joelianto Noegroho, collaborated with Andra Matin on the landscape design.

The house is accessed from a modest entrance in Jalan Sari Dewi, a narrow lane in the town of Seminyak, and thence by an open-to-sky passage that emerges in a spacious water court. Turning sharply to the left on entering the compound, a broad timber walkway invites visitors to proceed along a diagonal route, over a shallow pond, to the principal pavilion.

The loose wooden planks resonate when crossing the bridge to the living area. Small round gray pebbles glitter beneath the surface of the pond, and the gentle splash of water cascading down a vertical green wall forms part of the magical experience on entering. The central feature of the garden is a majestic frangipani tree that drapes gracefully over the 25-meter blue-green lap pool. A raised timber terrace equipped with rattan reclining chairs overlooks the pool. Water is a key component of the design and the garden draws inspiration from the traditional *rumah air* (water palace). There is utter silence in the garden except for the gentle splash of fountains and the murmur of the wind.

The unique feature of the house is the structure of the main pavilion, which combines the artistic legacy of Bali with sound building technology. The basic concrete-framed structure is overlaid with a steel mesh trellis and steel louvers, the geometry of the steel "veil" having been inspired by the branches of the tropical frangipani. The pavilion is open-sided at the ground-floor level, with a glazed upper floor that, sheltered by the protective metal screen, has the option of using air-conditioners or natural ventilation. By contrast, the smaller master bedroom pavilion is topped by a densely planted green roof, and a screen of hanging vines acts as a solar filter, thereby reducing insolation. The private realm is quite separate from the more public areas of the house.

Pages 34–5 The signature roof form is instantly recognizable in this seminal new Balinese house.

Above A "curtain" of green vegetation shades the master bedroom pavilion.

Right and far right A steel mesh "veil," inspired by the leaves of the frangipani tree, protects the house from solar insolation.

The extraordinarily beautiful Joelianto House is the outcome of Andra Matin's imagination. It is a design of such sensitivity that it confirms him as one of the most accomplished designers of his generation. His architecture has assurance and composure that can be compared favorably with the best in the world. Art works in the larger pavilion complement the design and include "Sofa Artwork Puzzle" by Yu Swant Ashoro.

Andra Matin explains it thus: "Indonesian culture is like an unpolished diamond, and this allows many possibilities—one has the freedom to put one's imagination to work. Contemporary Indonesian architecture reflects a huge number of cultures on the hundreds of islands in the archipelago and balances local conditions and global inspiration."[1]

[1] Quoted in Bert de Muynk and Kim Sang-Ho, "New Indonesian Tropical Architecture/Affordable+Green Public Housing," in SPACE voice maker, ESpace, edition 498, May 2009.

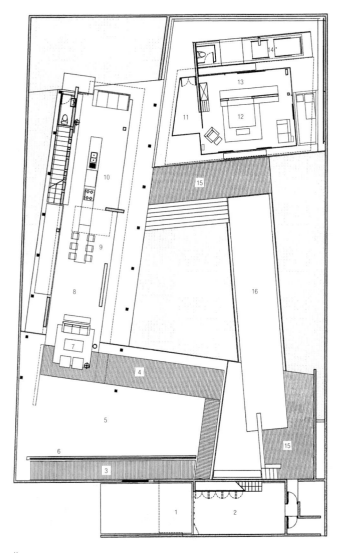

Key

1	Carport	9	Dining area
2	Garage	10	Pantry
3	Entrance path	11	Foyer
4	Deck	12	Master bedroom
5	Pond	13	Master bathroom
6	Water wall	14	Master shower
7	Living room	15	Pool deck
8	Foyer	16	Swimming pool

N

0   5   10 meters

Left The entrance to the court-yard viewed across an enchanting water garden.

Far left Ground floor plan.

Above The galley kitchen with the living area beyond.

Below left The main house viewed from the swimming pool.

Below right A diagonal flight of stairs ascends to the veranda of the master bedroom.

Above left The open-to-sky bath-room and toilet at the rear of the master bedroom.

Left The narrow entrance to the house precedes the dramatic space explosion of space in the water court.

Above Water cascades down a vertical wall in the courtyard.

W house

JAKARTA
ARCHITECT: ANDRA MATIN
ANDRAMATIN

Andra Matin first came to the attention of an International audience with the publication of his award-winning design for the LeBoYe Graphic office in Jakarta. It was one of the first projects to emerge from his fledgling practice and immediately set him apart as a designer of considerable skill.[1]

The W House has similarly generated much interest and has been published in a number of journals, including *GA Houses* (Japan)[2] and *SKALA* (Indonesia).[3] The owner is a businessman, restaurateur and publisher whose bookshelves reveal a keen interest in architecture and design, with titles by all the leading exponents.

The house is located in the garden of his parents' house and shares a striking green-blue swimming pool surrounded by luxuriant tropical vegetation. Approached up a gentle ramp from the car porch, a processional route through the surrounding trees gradually reveals the form of the dwelling. The upper floor is expressed as a timber louvered box with a wide oversailing roof, which "floats" above the more transparent ground floor. The most immediate visible quality of the house is its interlocking geometry.

The shifting geometry of the plan is readily apparent when moving through the ground floor. The plan is essentially linear, but the spatial choreography is refined, with framed views to the exterior. External walls at ground-floor level are sliding or hinged glass doors and perforated metal panels that can be opened so that the entire ground level can be connected to the garden. There is a particularly entrancing view from the kitchen through the dining room to the living area and beyond to the garden. In-between spaces and gentle ramps are elements of Andra Matin's architectural vocabulary that appear in other houses he has designed and here, in the W House, they are fully exploited.

The principal route to the upper floor is a 900-mm-wide smooth polished concrete ramp that ascends the south façade and is expressed on the façade as a rectangular glass and steel mesh "tube." The glass enclosure to the ramp is designed with vertical slots to permit permanent ventilation, while the upper floor is encircled by a double-skin wall with glass internal walls protected by an external "skin" of horizontal timber louvers. The first-floor accommodation includes a generous master bedroom suite, a guest bedroom and a study with an external terrace.

Materials employed include off-form concrete walls, gray polished cement floors and timber. Stainless steel and a gray laminate material are used for kitchen fittings and base units. The house is entirely naturally ventilated, but with the option of using air-conditioning in the bedrooms.

The W House is one of the seminal houses constructed in Indonesia in the last decade. Its robust form provokes memories of the Short Farmhouse in New South Wales by Glen Murcutt, and the honest expression of materials is a reminder of the tactile appeal of Geoffrey Bawa's houses in Sri Lanka. A haven of seclusion and calm in a hectic city, the relative simplicity of the form belies the complexity of the interior and the intensity of ideas embodied in the overall design.

Pages 42–3 The roof soars above the outdoor living space.

Top The garden terrace.

Above A lightwell in the center of the plan brings daylight into the middle of the house.

Opposite The "green wall" on the boundary of the site is covered in vegetation, which reduces solar radiation.

[1] I visited the Graphic Office in 1999 and, subsequently, as the editor of *SPACE* magazine, Singapore, I published it in edition 2002/02, pp. 90–3.

[2] Winfred Hutabaret, in *GA Houses* 112, Japan, October 2009; also in *Elle Decoration*, UK, October 2009; and in *GA Houses* 100, Japan, September 2009.

[3] Winner of SKALA Award, Indonesia, November 2007.

Above Glazed walls slide aside to create a living room that is contiguous with the outdoor spaces.

Left Horizontal louvers maintain a cool interior in the guest bedroom.

Below The house has deep overhangs and shaded interiors—the essence of a dwelling in the tropics.

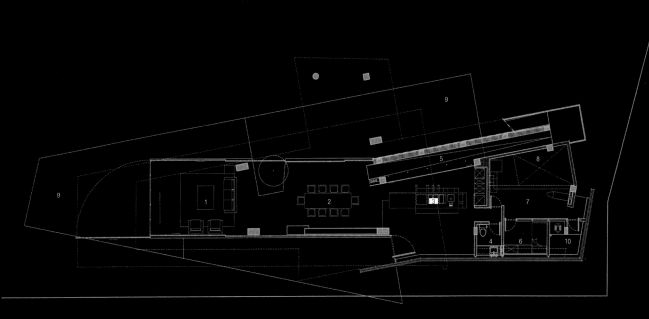

Key
1 Living room
2 Dining room
3 Pantry
4 Powder room
5 Ramp
6 Maid's room
7 Service area
8 Drying area
9 Terrace
10 Maid's bathroom

0   5   10 meters

Top Ground floor plan.

Left View of the kitchen, a slightly spartan space with an off-form concrete ceiling and polished cement floors.

Above center and right A narrow ramp ascends to the first floor.

bea house

JAKARTA

ARCHITECTS: Antony Liu & Ferry Ridwan

Antony Liu and Ferry Ridwan Architects

The Bea House is the home of the architect Antony Liu and his family. It is located adjacent to a golf course in the western Jakarta suburb of Tangerang. The single-story house, flanked by pine trees, is an extraordinarily pure expression of restrained modernism. It has a strong linear plan form, with a circulation spine that separates the "served" and "servant" spaces, which extend from the front to the rear of the dwelling, and terminate in a living/dining area that overlooks the golf course. Running parallel with the house is a garden and recreation area.

The entrance to the house is by way of a gentle ramp alongside a smooth off-form concrete wall and thence into an outer courtyard with a shallow pond within a gray split river stone and pebble garden. There is an almost surreal atmosphere as intermittent columns of white mist spurt from nozzles set in the ground plane. Approaching the entrance lobby, the gray monochrome palette is softened by vertical *bangkirai* timber louvers, a material that is repeated on the underside of the shallow-pitched wide overhanging roof. Within the minimalist lobby is a space to greet visitors and for shoes to be removed and placed in concealed cupboards.

Parallel with the northern boundary of the house is a linear fish pond and, behind a concealing wall, the maidspace together with wet and dry kitchens. The family accommodation takes a linear form, with the living/dining room, the guest room, two children's rooms and the master bedroom suite arranged as a series of linked spaces opening to a wide shaded veranda overlooking the garden. As one penetrates deeper into the private domain, there is increasing security. The master bedroom suite has a very private walled courtyard with a timber pergola, outdoor shower and Japanese-style wooden bathtub.

The name of the house, Bea, is an abbreviation of "beautiful," a word that has special significance for the deeply religious architect who sees God's hand in the creation of a family home. Liu's earliest architectural influences were the masters of modern architecture, among them Frank Lloyd Wright and Mies van der Rohe, but as a result of his travels with Arsitek Muda Indonesia to Japan and Europe he has also been captivated by the work of Tadao Ando, Kengo Kuma, Kerry Hill and Peter Zumthor. The architectural

Pages 48–9 The sheer elegance of the Bea House is best appreciated at dusk.

Above The entrance courtyard, with its subtle landscape of gray stone, mist and dark water.

language of the house has a distinct signature that incorporates modernism and "minimalism." The materials used throughout the house are a subtle combination of gray off-form concrete and galvanized steel, with open mesh walls balanced by timber louvers and *bangkirai* timber decks. Details are carefully considered and finely executed. Against an essentially monochrome backcloth, there are sudden splashes of color: a deep ultramarine swimming pool, a gorgeous bougainvillea tree and lush green landscape. The architect is also an artist and there are a number of his works, mostly Mel Gibson caricatures from the "Mad Max 3" movie, carried out in the 1980s, hung around the house.

Antony Liu explains of the work of Antony Liu and Ferry Ridwan Architects: "We want to find purity, we eschew traditional forms of architecture and our intention is to create architecture that is unrepentantly modern in appearance. We aim to achieve calm relaxed modern architecture. Each project doesn't have to be radically different from a previous design but we seek to make it more refined. Minimalism is an answer to some of the problems posed by the climate; the wide overhanging roof is intended to avoid excessive sun, light, and rain and act as basic elements in our exploration of tropical architecture." He goes on: "It has been a tough job to educate clients in this concept, as there is a common misconception about what minimalism means. People think it is about style, but it isn't—it is a way of living and thinking."[1]

Along the southern boundary of the garden there is a long, shallow steel and concrete ramp through a bamboo grove that forms a green tunnel leading to a viewing platform, with a panoramic view over the golf course. Beneath the viewing platform is accommodation for two large dogs kept for security purposes. The landscape of the garden, designed by Hujan Mas, blurs the borders with the golf course so that the two appear to conjoin and the house enjoys "borrowed" scenery. In November 2009, Antony Liu and Ferry Ridwan Architects received an IAI Award for the design of the Bea House.

[1] See Bert de Muynck, "Regional Architecture Confronting with Indonesian Tropical Climate," in SPACE voice maker, ESpace, May 25, 2009.

Above The unwavering linear route from the entrance lobby to the living room.

Right A narrow fish pond runs along the northern boundary.

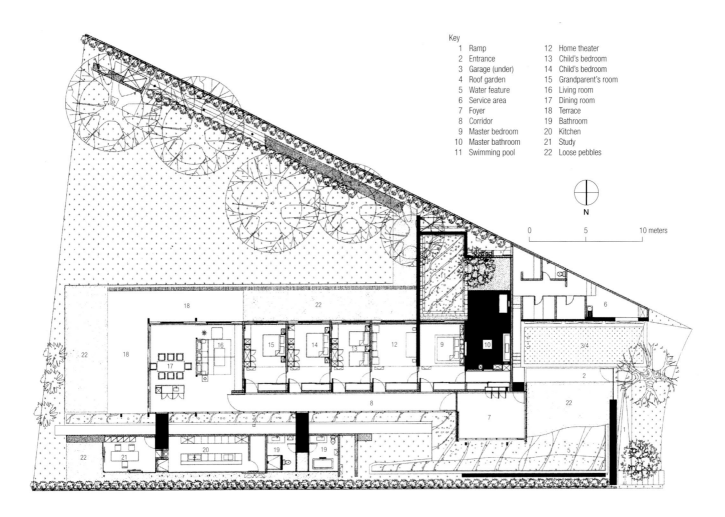

Key
1	Ramp	12	Home theater
2	Entrance	13	Child's bedroom
3	Garage (under)	14	Child's bedroom
4	Roof garden	15	Grandparent's room
5	Water feature	16	Living room
6	Service area	17	Dining room
7	Foyer	18	Terrace
8	Corridor	19	Bathroom
9	Master bedroom	20	Kitchen
10	Master bathroom	21	Study
11	Swimming pool	22	Loose pebbles

N

0   5   10 meters

Top Ground floor plan.

Above A bougainvillea tree and a plunge pool are the colorful focus of a Japanese-inspired courtyard.

Opposite above The warmth of timber contrasts with the polished cement floor in the entrance lobby.

Right The courtyard accessed from the master bedroom is a delightfully private space.

Far right There is a mysterious quality to the spaces along the northern boundary.

Left and below left Views of the living room terrace.

Below The entrance lobby viewed from the linear fish pond.

Above The low pitch of the roof is expressed within the living room.

Right Mature trees flank the entrance to the house.

ridwan kamil
house

BANDUNG
ARCHITECT: M. RIDWAN KAMIL
URBANE ARCHITECTS

M. Ridwan Kamil gained his architectural degree at the Institute of Technology in Bandung (ITB), and in 1994 he spent a semester at the National University of Singapore, where he attended lectures on urban design. Later, he worked for HOK in New York and then went on to earn his Masters degree in Urban Design at the University of California, Berkeley, where Professor Allan B. Jacobs taught courses in the Department of City and Regional Planning. After Graduate School, he interned with SOM in California. He now teaches at his alma mater, ITB, and is principal of Urbane Architects, a practice he set up in June 2004 that is involved in major master planning work.

The Ridwan Kamil House is located on a trapezoidal-shaped site in Bandung, and the U-shaped plan of the house encloses an internal courtyard—a typical Javanese urban morphology. It is situated close to the architect's mother's dwelling and his house provides a space for the extended family to gather. The house is entered from the street into a single-story covered veranda inspired by Dutch colonial architecture and thence to the living room where *merbau* timber from sustainable sources is used on the ceiling and floor. The dining room, kitchen and living room all look into the central courtyard, which offers many advantages. "So much light enters from both sides that we don't need artificial lighting during the daytime," says Ridwan.[1] In addition, the prevailing breezes, cooled by the water in the courtyard, contribute to the coolness of the interior. At the heart of the house is a small amphitheater for family entertainment.

At the top of the dwelling are the master bedroom suite and the architect's library and study. In the master bedroom, a green glass shelf contains a collection of miniatures of some of the buildings he has admired during his travels, and in the bedroom's sitting area is a painting of New York City's skyline by Ian Mulyana, a Bandung artist, titled "Manhattan Green."

The split-level house is purposely designed to create secure areas so that the bedrooms and children's rooms are isolated and accessed by ramps and stairs.

The most striking feature of the house is its external "skin." Sometimes referred to as Rumah Botol (Bottle House), the façade is made from 30,000 recycled Red Bull bottles. The high-caffeine beverage, sold in most parts of the world in distinctive blue and silver cans, is retailed in Indonesia in brown bottles. "These bottles litter the streets," Ridwan explains. "We don't have a recycling system, so when I

Pages 58–9 The extraordinary Ridwan Kamil House, clad in 30,000 recycled bottles.

Above Daylight enters the central courtyard and prevailing breezes permit the house to be naturally ventilated.

decided to build a house for my family, I thought I would make them a significant part of the exterior and interior. I'm a proponent of recycling."[2] This is an inventive method of recycling as most of the bottles were scavenged from refuse dumps in Bandung, Tasikmalaya and Cirebon over a six-month period. The metal caps had been discarded, so the architect designed wooden tops for all 30,000 bottles.

The bottles form 60 percent of the façade, and especially in the early morning and late evening they filter light from east and west. The architect had a gut feeling that the bottles would provide additional insulation, and subsequent research by a student in the Department of Architecture at Parahyangan Catholic University in Bandung proved him right. "The research revealed that somehow heat was captured inside the bottles and not transferred into the space inside, especially when there is a gap between the external bottle wall and an inner glass wall like in all of the upper areas.... This gap gives you an insulating system that totally stops the sun's heat from transferring inside."[3] The result is that most of the rooms in the completely air-conditioning free house remain a comfortable 75 degrees.

Basically, the architect designed on-site, handing the contractor dozens of hand-drawn sketches and working drawings. "I came," he recalls, "I imagined, and I drew.... The best part was when I got the big idea of what to do with thousands of recycled bottles. I was experimenting.... I tested many ways to construct using the bottles. They add a unique quality to my home."[4]

The architect declares that the outcome of the experiment is overwhelmingly positive. "Clients are more confident working with me when they see my design philosophy applied in my own home. The spirit of recycling also gets into their thinking in a revolutionary way.... Some of my clients are now starting to think about using recycled materials."[5]

[1–3] Susan Sheehan, "Designers' Own Homes: Ridwan Kamil," *Architectural Digest*, Conde Nast Digital, September 2009.
[4, 5] Ridwan Kamil, "Advice on Designing Your Own Home," *Architectural Digest*, Conde Nast Digital, September 2009.

Above The external "skin" of recycled bottles viewed from the architect's study.

Above right A louvered timber screen filters the west light entering the master bedroom from the central courtyard.

Right Ground floor plan.

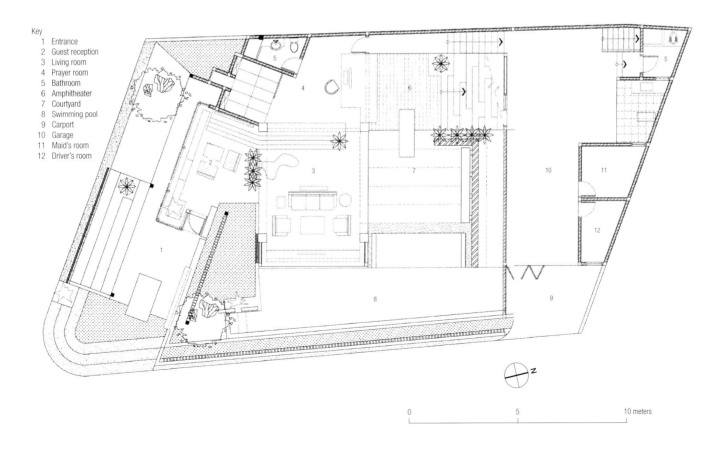

0   5   10 meters

Left A gentle ramp gives access to the children's bedroom.

Right and far right Elegant internal and external details of the unusual façade material.

Below The courtyard at the heart of the plan visually connects the major living spaces.

Key
1 Entrance
3 Living room
7 Courtyard
8 Swimming pool
10 Garage
12 Driver's room
13 Dining room
16 Children's room
21 Study

Left The recycled bottles create a tactile façade.

Below left Section drawing.

Right The entrance to the house is from an open veranda facing the street.

Below The brown glass façade glows in the evening.

k house

BANDUNG
ARCHITECT: TAN TJIANG AY

Tan Tjiang Ay was born in Central Java in 1940. He studied at the Institute of Technology Bandung from 1958 to 1960 at a time when the works of the twentieth-century "masters," Frank Lloyd Wright and Le Corbusier, were being introduced into a curriculum that was modeled on Delft University of Technology in the Netherlands. He was one year ahead of Romo Mangun, who would later become an architect/priest of considerable stature. The architecture of Walter Gropius and Alvar Aalto greatly influenced Tan in these formative years. In 1960, Tan transferred from ITB to Parahyangan Catholic University (1960 to 1968) to complete his studies, and was in private practice between 1968 and 1972 before taking up a partnership with Lampiri Indonesia Architects for the next eight years. In 1980, he resumed his own practice, concentrating on the design of private dwellings.

I first met Tan Tjiang Ay in 1993 when researching my book, *The Tropical Asian House*, and subsequently I published his family residence in Bandung. Now in his seventieth year, he is a doyen of the profession in Indonesia, and his work is much admired by a younger generation. A committed

modernist, he continues to refine details and experiment with structure and form. He produces exceptionally well-mannered modern architecture that thrills by its adherence to the Vitruvian principles of commodity, firmness and delight.

The K House, sometimes referred to as "The House in the Highlands," is located in the hills to the north of Bandung and is the latest in an oeuvre of residential projects that have won Tan wide respect in the architectural profession in Indonesia and further afield in Asia. He has an unerring ability to know when "enough is enough" so that his designs are always clean, precise essays in a modern architectural language, unencumbered by excessive features or unnecessary decoration. A feature of all of Tan's designs is his masterly expertise in inserting a house into the landscape with minimal damage to the ecosystem. It is a rare skill that I associate with other acclaimed architects in Asia, such as Geoffrey Bawa and Kerry Hill.

The architectural program of the K House is split into four parts. Two pavilions are located on the lower slopes of the valley while a third pavilion is set on the higher contours.

Pages 68–9 The K House nestles in the hills to the north of Bandung.

Left The east-facing façade overlooks the arrival courtyard.

Right The imposing entrance to the house.

Far right The living room veranda gives magnificent views of the valley to the east.

Below View to the east from the gym at the upper level of the site.

Outbuildings are even higher up the hillside, accessed by a steep path. The house is approached from the north along the side of a valley. The grass-crete driveway traverses the slope, dropping gently to the small plateau on which the main living accommodation is located. The larger of the two pavilions on the lower slopes contains the living and dining rooms, with a veranda looking east over the valley and with a rear patio that catches the late afternoon sun. The master bedroom suite on the upper floor also enjoys a view to the east and a view into a double-height void that serves to reduce solar insolation. A sub-basement garage is entered from the lowest level of the site.

The smaller of the two pavilions contains the maidspace and two additional bedrooms. Both pavilions are just one room wide, insuring they can benefit from natural ventilation, while the pitched roof has overhanging eaves to shade

the walls and shed monsoon rainfall. The third pavilion, on the upper slopes, is a glass box that contains a gym and relaxation space, with much of the external wall in the form of glazed doors that can be thrown open to give an unrestricted view of the valley to the east and the hills to the northeast.

The simplicity of the K House plans is revealing. The resolution seems to be effortlessly achieved, but this very simplicity is the mark of a genius who is able to distill a complex brief into a remarkably clear plan form. Tan's mastery of tectonics is exemplary: the two main pavilions are joined in a manner that expresses their different purpose but, simultaneously, that they are part of a whole. The hillside has been relatively undisturbed by the building operations and the result, as with all of Tan's houses, is a calm ensemble of forms that rests easily in the landscape.

Above Bandung's altitude insures that the living room enjoys wonderful cooling breezes.

Above right The patio at the rear of the house.

Right The marvelous interplay of internal volumes is typical of Tan Tjiang Ay's designs.

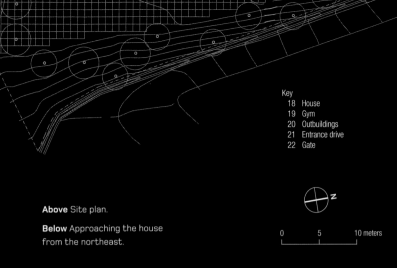

Key
18 House
19 Gym
20 Outbuildings
21 Entrance drive
22 Gate

N

Above Site plan.

Below Approaching the house
from the northeast.

0   5   10 meters

Right The view from the entrance courtyard toward the house entrance.

Below A wonderful panoramic view of the wooded valley below the house.

tukad balian
house

SIDAKARYA, BALI
ARCHITECTS: ANTONY LIU & FERRY RIDWAN
ANTONY LIU AND FERRY RIDWAN ARCHITECTS

Antony Liu Budiwihardja was born in Jakarta in 1967. He studied architecture at Universitas Tarumanagara in Jakarta, from where he graduated in 1991. He first found employment with PT Pakar Cipta Graha in Jakarta. His business partner, Ferry Ridwan, who was born in Bandung in 1970, is a 1993 graduate of the same university and he, too, commenced his architectural career with PT Pakar Cipta Graha. In 1996, they resigned to form Antony Liu and Ferry Ridwan Architects. The practice has now established a formidable reputation for its design of exotic resorts, including The Balé hotel, Nusa Dua, and the Oasis 1 and 2, also in Bali. Liu and Ridwan are both active members of Arsitek Muda Indonesia.

The Tukad Balian House is the Bali home and design studio of the acclaimed American landscape architect Karl Princic and his Indonesian wife Dhea. The house is located on a long rectangular plot of land on the southern fringe of Denpasar beside the road leading to the coastal resort of Sanur. The site was previously an agricultural holding and is surrounded by paddy fields. The rectilinear profile of the house distinguishes it from its neighbors and from its surroundings. In the tropics, one searches for a place where there is a breath of wind and here, on the outskirts of the built-up area, there is a cooling breeze.

As a direct consequence of the site configuration, the design has a linear plan form. The plot has been simply zoned, with the front half of the site facing the highway allocated to a design office, and the quieter rear half allocated to residential use. Both the design office and the residence are accessed from a single entrance at the center of the northern façade. Directly ahead in the garden is a single huge *kapok* tree that was on the site and which forms the fulcrum of the plan. The entrance lobby bifurcates at this point, with office visitors turning left to the reception area and visitors to the residence to the right. Timber slats emphasize the roof above the entrance.

The house-cum-studio is a single-story steel-framed transparent glass box with "I" columns and a monopitch roof. The principal rooms face into a linear garden that boasts a 32-meter black *candi* stone swimming pool. All the rooms in the residence have floor-to-ceiling frameless sliding glazed doors on the south elevation, and when the occasion demands they can be pushed aside to allow family and guests to move freely from the interior to the poolside.

In arriving at the simple form, the architects acknowledge a debt to the Californian case study steel houses of the 1940s and 1950s. Karl Princic had introduced them to his favorite steel-frame houses and these were the inspiration

Pages 76–7 The house is an elegant design in the sprit of the Californian case study steel houses of the 1950s.

Left The cool modern light-filled open-plan dining and living room beneath an inclined ceiling.

Right A linear concrete wall delineates public and private areas.

Far right The entrance lobby focuses on a single large kapok tree that was on the site.

Below The swimming pool deck beneath the kapok tree.

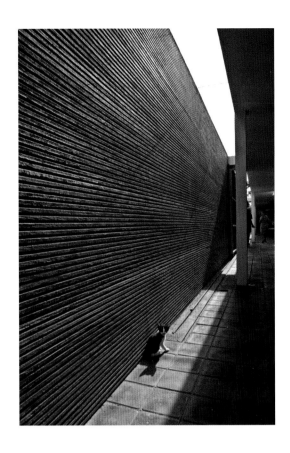

for the project. Having grown up in Southern California during the 1960s, Princic had been both consciously and subconsciously influenced by the modern architecture of that time. The houses designed in the latter stages of the program by Killingsworth, Brady and Smith were, for him, the embodiment of cool architecture. Together with Liu and Ridwan, he set out to adapt these concepts to the tropics and the design of the house became a close collaboration.

The house is correctly orientated for the tropics, with the narrow elevations facing east and west. Surrounded by a high concrete wall, it is horizontally stratified from north to south. The north elevation is solid and projects a sense of enclosure and privacy. A second parallel layer contains the maidspace, driver's accommodation, private carport and services, with provision for a guard dog. A third layer contains the glass box and a hint of openness, with glimpses of the garden beyond, while a fourth and fifth layer reveal a broad sheltered veranda and, finally, the openness of the modern landscaped south-facing walled garden and pool. Large clay pots are carefully located to terminate strategic views, and an abstract sculpture by a Balinese artist is placed at the end of the swimming pool.

The residence is separated from the office, conference area and design studio by a screen of frosted glass doors. The doors can be opened to extend the apparent length of the garden or closed to give the house greater privacy or to permit an office function on the lawn. The office has its own courtyard, enhanced by a wide-spreading ficus tree.

Given his Californian origins, the client, Karl Princic, wanted to work "in the context of modern architecture which is simple and restful,"[1] and his collaboration with Antony Liu and Ferry Ridwan Architects was clearly mutually beneficial in this respect. The home they collectively designed is a spectacular, calm, uncluttered modernist place employing cool white planes and volumes and contrasting openness and enclosure. There is a corresponding silence within the sheltered garden. The modern language continues in the cool interior where, in the living room, there is a spectacular painting by the Indonesian artist Hanafi.

Antony Liu and Ferry Ridwan Architects has received numerous awards for its completed projects, including an IAI Award in 2002 for the design of The Balé hotel project at Nusa Dua Bali; an IAI Award in 2006 for the Bukit Golf Clubhouse at Cimanggis; the Conrad Wedding Chapel in Nusa Dua, Bali (in collaboration with Andra Matin); and in November 2009, an IAI Award for the Bea House in Serpong, Tangerang. In the role of landscape architect, Karl Princic worked with Liu and Ridwan on Oasis 1 and 2, The Balé hotel and the Bukit Golf Clubhouse.

[1] E-mail correspondence with Karl Princic, April 2, 2010.

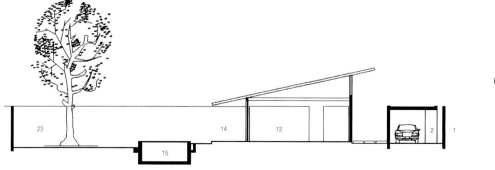

Key
1 Entrance
2 Garage
12 Dining area
14 Terrace
15 Swmming pool
23 Garden

Left A simple garden seat alongside the pool.

Right Ground floor plan.

Below The entrance to the owner's design office that is located alongside the dwelling.

Below right The entrance drive to the house and office.

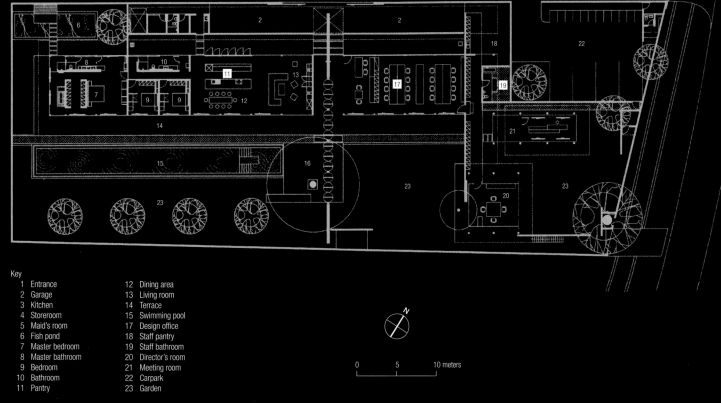

Key
1 Entrance
2 Garage
3 Kitchen
4 Storeroom
5 Maid's room
6 Fish pond
7 Master bedroom
8 Master bathroom
9 Bedroom
10 Bathroom
11 Pantry
12 Dining area
13 Living room
14 Terrace
15 Swimming pool
17 Design office
18 Staff pantry
19 Staff bathroom
20 Director's room
21 Meeting room
22 Carpark
23 Garden

0   5   10 meters

pondok indah

JAKARTA
ARCHITECT: RENÉ TAN
RT+Q ARCHITECTS

house

René Tan was born in Malaysia and attended Penang Free School (1977–83), the *alma mater* of two other notable Southeast Asian architects, Ken Yeang and Chan Soo Khian. He then studied at Yale University, from 1983 to 1987, where he began as a music major with the intention of becoming a concert pianist, but eventually graduated with a Bachelor of Arts in music and architecture. He went on to pursue graduate studies at Princeton (1987–90), where he was awarded his Master in Architecture.

Among the notable teachers he encountered at Princeton were Ralph Lerner, the Dean, and Michael Graves. From Ralph Lerner he learnt about "attitude," "rigor," "discipline" and "commitment"; Michael Graves taught him the value of history, plan-making and the "necessity of drawing." The two professors represented for Tan the very best aspects of a Princeton education. Asked to single out practitioners who have influenced his architecture, he identifies Oscar Niemeyer (whom he admires for the boldness of his forms), Louis Kahn (for the rigor of his forms) and Le Corbusier (for the fearlessness of his forms). René now teaches two days each month at Hong Kong University School of Architecture.

The Pondok Indah House was designed by Tan and his colleague Jonathan Quek for an Indonesian businessman who is an art collector and avid golfer. The house is situated on the fringe of the Pondok Indah Golf Course and overlooks a water obstacle in front of the twelfth green.

The house is approached from a spacious vehicle court up a slight incline and a broad flight of stairs to the entrance foyer that incorporates good *feng shui*. A sharp right turn followed by a sharp left turn reveals a dramatic vista along a north–south axis. The axis is accentuated by a linear water garden culminating in a view over an infinity swimming pool to the golf course.

The plan is essentially an H form, with two linear blocks on either side of the central north–south axis connected by a bridge at first-floor level. The eastern wing consists of a spa, AV room, breakfast room, dry kitchen, vertical circulation, sitting room and a huge double-height formal dining room with 7.2-meter-high sliding doors, extending to an external deck at ground level. The western wing

Pages 84–5 The elegant house is seen at its best at sunset.

Right A transparent glazed bridge connects the two wings of the house at first-floor level.

Above The terrace at the rear of the house overlooks a water hazard on the Pondok Indah Golf Course.

Right A timber deck connects the eastern and western wings at ground level.

Opposite The impressive two-story formal dining room with the library/gallery beyond.

Opposite far right Ground floor plan.

consists of a music room and a formal living room at the same level; a timber deck connects the two wings. At the end of the western wing is a waterfall and a fitness court at basement level.

At first-floor level, the east wing contains two bedrooms and a family room, while the west wing contains the master bedroom suite. A refined glazed bridge housing a gallery, a library and separate study rooms for parents and children connects the two wings. Natural ventilation is introduced utilizing the Venturi principle.

The house is a truly dramatic composition. The configuration of the site is challenging, yet helps to create a distinctive plan form; it is a spatial composition of consummate artistry. The junctions are articulated

brilliantly and materials are chosen with care. The external landscape complements the mood of each space and the architect created a water garden that is very much in the spirit of Javanese palaces. The dining room and the formal living area are both huge, yet the house also has a sense of intimacy and calm.

Paintings by artists of international renown punctuate the route through the house, among them "Institut de France" by Bernard Buffet, "Dancers" by Fernando Botero, "Lovers and Bouquet" by Marc Chagall and "Cultural Revolution: Eternal Halo" by Wang Guangyi. There is also an oil painting on a panel depicting "Three Horses" by Lee Man Fong and a bronze sculpture in front of the travertine entrance wall by Li Chen entitled "Pure Land."

N

0   5   10 meters

Left A generous corridor leads from the entrance foyer to the living area.

Above The exquisitely detailed gallery and library "bridge" connecting the two wings.

Above left Looking southwest across the swimming pool from the dining room terrace.

Far left, center and right The house has numerous refined details.

Above The impressive double-height dining room opens onto the pool terrace.

Right The guardhouse.

sitok
srengenge house

Eko Agus Prawoto was born in 1958 and is a graduate of Gajah Mada University in his home city of Yogyakarta. He went on to acquire a Masters degree at the Berlage Institute in the Netherlands, where Herman Hertzberger headed the architecture department. Later, he worked for a period with the renowned Indian architect Balkrishna V. Doshi in Ahmedabad before returning to Yogyakarta, where in 1985 he helped set up the architecture department at Duta Wacana Christian University. He rose to be head of the department. One of his students was Budi Pradono, whose work appears elsewhere in this book. Today, he is Head of the Industrial Design Department at the university and also runs his own architectural practice.

Prawoto's mentor at Gajah Mada University was Yusuf Bilyarta Mangunwijaya (Romo Mangun), a famed Javanese polymath who was a writer and priest in addition to being a gifted architect. Prawoto studied under Mangunwijaya in 1980 and had a close relationship with him for almost two decades after that. Mangunwijaya stressed the importance of spending money on training first and materials second, a strategy adhered to by his disciple. "He wanted to empower the people," recalls Prawoto, "by giving them a skill that would last beyond any one project."[1] That accumulated knowledge informs Prawoto's attitude to construction. "I have learned a lot from local builders and carpenters who know best how to use materials," he says. "Roma Mangun was an activist. His architecture was not only about aesthetics but how to create job opportunities with local materials. I have pursued the same ideals," adds Prawoto.

Prawoto is keen to point out that the architectural discourse in Jakarta is very different to that in Yogyakarta, where budgets are generally lower. "Almost 75 percent of the wealth of the country passes through the capital and clearly that has an effect on architecture. In Yogyakarta, architects are required to 'do more with less.'" Prawoto makes a subtle distinction saying, "In Jakarta architects produce avant-garde architecture, here we produce alternative architecture." He is recognized for his contemporary designs that utilize local materials— bamboo, stone, coconut palm wood, terracotta—that are sustainable, often recycled and highly suitable for regions prone to geological disturbances and flooding. The Sitok Srengenge House is the home of a 45-year-old poet who, in 2000, was cited by *Asiaweek* magazine as one of the twenty "leaders for the millennium in society and culture" in Asia. He and his wife, Farah Maulida, move between their Jakarta home and their house in Bangunjiwo on the outskirts of Yogya, staying on average for two weeks every month in their forest retreat.

Sitok acquired the site when looking for a recycled door for another project. A friend directed him to a small workshop about 50 meters away. He did not find the door he was seeking but he spotted the site and immediately "fell in love with the valley." There was, he said, "a mythological connection" with the site also. There is an old saying that if you can find your way blindfolded between two banyan trees in the southern square of a *kraton* (palace), your wish will be granted. Shortly before finding the site, he did precisely this and almost immediately found the site. The land price was not too high and he and his wife bought it and appointed Prawoto, who produced plans and a maquette, but they could not afford to build for two years.

There was only one place on the site where there were no trees—a small clearing—so that is where the house is located. The dining pavilion and staff accommodations are located to the north at the foot of a slope. The house is a "work in progress," and they plan to build two more pavilions to house a prayer room and a library.

Pages 94–5 The house is approached through an amazing avenue of trees.

Opposite and above A blue-painted timber bridge across a shallow pond gives access to the house.

Prawoto explains the design thus. The idea was not to have a compact house, for they regard the house not as just the building but occupying the whole of the 1.3-ha site. They live a sort of nomadic lifestyle, moving from place to place on the site. The dining room is actually located about 40 meters from the main house in a deep valley, and to take breakfast they descend a flight of steps through the forest. Javanese houses allow you to move around, so the concept is very traditional. Modern houses are, unfortunately, often determined by more pragmatic considerations and rooms are labeled with specific functions.

The house is located at the end of an unmade track, past a century-old aristocratic house with a *joglo*-style roof. The route changes to a path of "stepping stones" through the trees, passes over a rattan bridge that spans a water retention pond, and then down stone steps to a small amphitheater that precedes the dwelling. Visitors then cross a blue wooden bridge over a *koi* pond to an ever-open door, at which point shoes must be removed. The route to the house is curiously like walking through an excavated ruin.

"A home should reflect one's culture but also empower the inhabitant," Prawoto says. "In the end, I just try to create a home for the soul." He favors a slow, deliberate approach, taking time to understand a client's requirements and produce appropriate designs. "I consider myself a midwife giving birth to homes that look like their parents," he says.

"Most people only build one house in their lifetime, so it is important to get it right. Too many architects are obsessed with showing themselves, whereas I want to show who and what is living there."

Mangunwijaya used to stress the need for buildings to be intimately related to their external environments. Prawoto agrees that "a building is not an autonomous object but also an emotional and social being." Prawoto has arrived at the same mantra as Geoffrey Bawa, and asserts that "not cutting down trees is important—always move a wall rather than cut down a tree." In a Prawoto-designed house, trees are often left standing, their branches protruding through holes cut in the roof.

The Sitok Srengenge House reminds the writer of other retreats: the Sri Lankan artist Laki Senanayake's house at Dhambula; the Malaysian landscape designer Tan Sek San's jungle house at Serendah, and in its openness it is akin to Geoffrey Bawa's Cinnamon Hill House at Lunuganga in Sri Lanka. Sitok wrote a poem for his wife about the house:

Above The first-floor living area is an open-to-sky room with views to the north.

Right The reception/dining area has immediate access to the north-facing garden.

HOME for Maulida

1

Within you who are always open to me
I find iron and wood structures,
stone formation and earthen mass,
like a house
A transit place without walls and doors
tempts me to enter you
from all directions

In the modest living room
old furniture await,
Faded textured wood
Each line keeping a memory

And in the study whose windows are always open,
I know, myriads of words
keep conversing with each other,
about the absent rain,
lying clouds,
visiting winds,
and lustful trees,
—intently listened to by the acacia trunks
nodded to by the mahogany leaves

2

When twilight has abated its desire
and we look towards north,
the shadows of mountains and gorges and cities
will elude our eyes
Only a lump of darkness
like a citadel of old
with the orange-gray light above it

An airplane always passes over there
Taking people traveling or returning home
like a bird hurrying to the nest before dark,
and sometimes we ask:
will there be among them a friend of ours
somebody who will stop by
just to extend greetings
and keep away ill feelings

When twilight has abated its desire
and we look towards north
the eyes are often trapped in the unreal
and yet we never grow wary of the transient

(Translated by Hasif Amini)

Opposite above left The entrance to the house frames views of the garden beyond.

Opposite above right Eye-catching details of the guest bedroom door and the roof structure.

Left The poet's study, with views to the reception/dining area beyond.

Above Dappled sunlight tumbles into the stairwell.

During the building process, the owners acquired two beautiful antique teak doors, only to discover that they were too tall for the ground floor. Undeterred, the architect turned this to advantage by incorporating them on the upper floor beneath the raised ceiling, with marvelous broken pediments above. The roof structure is a beautiful resolution of forces.

There are many other interesting details, such as the tiled walls in the bathrooms and a bamboo screen around the staircase. "Bamboo is an unusual material because no two pieces are the same, unlike steel tubes or aluminum extrusions," observes Prawoto. He reminds me of architect Bobby Mañosa in the Philippines, who has the same zeal as Prawoto for bamboo as a sustainable material.

"There are so many local traditions in Indonesia which has 350 ethnic groups, but because of the logic of industry you have to follow a standardized logic," says Prawoto. "It is important to give new energy to tradition," he remarks.

Two weeks before the author met him, Prawato had been a keynote speaker at a conference at the Bruno Zevi Foundation in Rome on the subject of "Frugal Architecture." His fellow discussants were Sarah Wigglesworth from the UK, Jorge Mario Jaurequi from Brazil, Nina Maritz from Namibia and Rural Studio from the USA.

Prawato is highly regarded in Indonesia and internationally for his sensitive architecture that incorporates local traditions and materials, and two of his projects were illustrated in *The Phaidon Atlas of 21st Century World Architecture* (2008), including one project in Papua. "The strength of architecture in Yogyakarta," he asserts, "is that we still care about neighbors and being tolerant." He is fortunate also in that his clients are nearly all artists, writers, musicians and poets, who generally have a social conscious and are respectful of nature. Prawato has also built up a considerable international reputation as a builder of installations, having directed projects in Japan, Korea and Italy.

[1] Eko Agus Prawato in conversation with the author, February 11, 2010.

Left Tactile detailing of a bamboo wall.

Below A sophisticated partition in the first-floor bathroom.

Right The house is approached on foot, there being no access for vehicles.

Above right The dining area is a pavilion located some 40 meters from the main house.

Right Ground-floor plan of the main house.

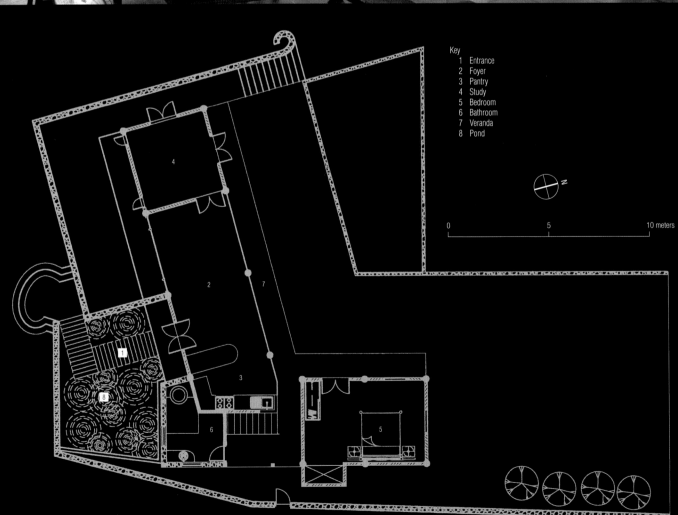

Key
1 Entrance
2 Foyer
3 Pantry
4 Study
5 Bedroom
6 Bathroom
7 Veranda
8 Pond

0   5   10 meters

BANDUNG
ARCHITECT: TAN TIK LAM
TAN TIK LAM ARCHITECTS

dago house no. 1

Tan Tik Lam was born in Bandung and trained at Para-hyangan Catholic University from 1988 to 1995. "The teachers were somewhat conservative," he recalls, "but the students were highly motivated and widely traveled."[1] Tan became a member of Arsitek Muda Indonesia (AMI), the student organization founded in 1989 by a group of young architects intent on promoting critical discussion of architecture. "AMI," he says, "opened our minds." He and his contemporaries—Denny Gondo, Ahmad Djuhara and Gregorius Supie Yolodi—formed the second generation of AMI or AMINext, as they are sometimes referred to.

Dago House No. 1 is approached up a narrow winding road that ascends one of the steep valleys to the north of Bandung. The road has a precipitous drop on one side and the site is a plateau hewn from the hillside. The house has a "longhouse" type of plan, stretching along the hillside from east to west, with the principal rooms facing south across a veranda and panoramic views over the city. It is what his father, the renowned architect Tan Tjiang Ay, refers to as "a railway station plan."[2] On the opposite side of the valley are farm terraces that supply fruit and vegetables to the city.

The entrance to the house is choreographed with great skill. An arrival court at the west end of the site, some seven meters below the house, gives access to the garage and domestic quarters. The house can be glimpsed on the hillside above an embankment of close-cropped grass. From the court, a four-meter-wide flight of stairs gently ascends the hillside behind a stone retaining wall. This is a compressed space that effectively delays the view down the valley. Arriving at the summit of the stairs, visitors turn 180 degrees to experience an exhilarating panorama of the city to the southwest and the mountains beyond.

The house is ideally orientated for the tropics. The rising sun falls upon the narrow east-facing elevation, and at its zenith the sun is almost directly overhead so that the broad south-facing veranda, with its pitched roof and low eaves, is in deep shade. At sunset, the owners sit on the west end of the terrace and view the valley across an infinity swimming pool. Bandung enjoys a far cooler climate than Jakarta, and it was here that the early Dutch colonizers escaped from the heat and humidity of the mosquito-infested swamps on which, for better or worse, they had sited the capital—

Top and above right A quiet court-yard accessed from the master bedroom.

Above A broad ramp ascends to the house entrance.

Right Section. drawing.

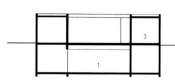

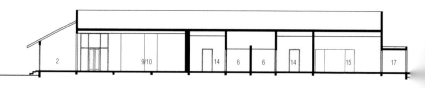

Batavia—in 1619. The house is well orientated to benefit from cooling breezes, and it is an added bonus that it rarely requires air-conditioning. The north elevation of the linear plan faces the hillside, and here a shaded landscaped courtyard has been created against a high retaining wall.

The striking topography creates a wonderful openness to the site. Sitting at an outdoor table on the terrace, the owners contemplate distant forested hills beyond the city, and narrow plumes of smoke drift from the farmers' controlled burning. There is deep silence, occasionally broken by the crow of a chicken or the distant growl of a motorbike climbing the road below. It is a laid-back place that connects with nature, and often the hillside is dramatically wreathed in clouds. Tan Tik Lam has designed a house that is restrained in its architectural language and admirably suited to the location.

[1] Tan Tik Lam in conversation with the author, October 27, 2009.
[2] Robert Powell, *The Tropical Asian House*, Singapore: Select Books, 1996, p. 68. Tan Tjiang Ay used this expression, in 1993, when referring to the design of his own house.

Below and right The entrance courtyard and stairs.

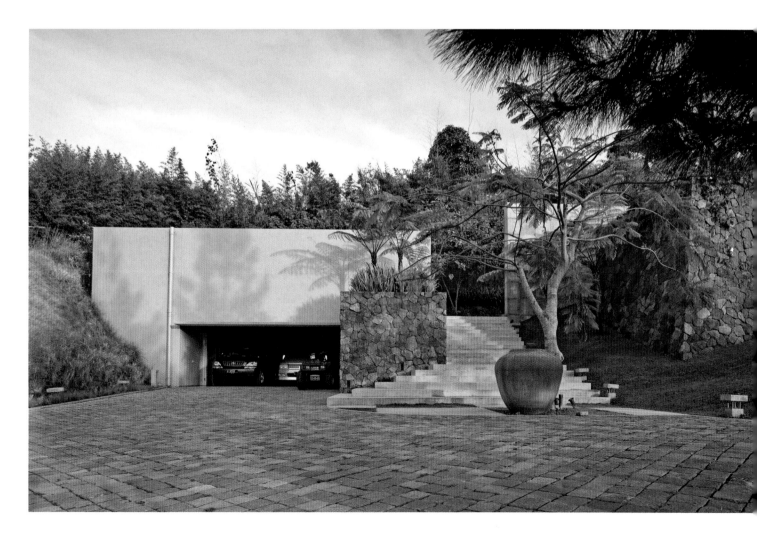

villa kalyani

TIBUBENANG, BALI
ARCHITECT: SEKAR WARNI
UTTARA INDONESIA

Sekar Warni was born in Jambi in Sumatra in 1971 and received her architectural training at Tarumanagara University in Jakarta, from which she graduated in 1994. After graduation, she worked as a project architect in Jakarta before setting up her own practice, Uttara Indonesia, in 2001.

Villa Kalyani is a vacation home in the village of Tibubenang, northwest of Denpasar, owned by Christophe Rougeron, a Singapore-based investment banker. Built on a long rectangular plot of land that was formerly rice paddy, this is a house designed for a sybaritic lifestyle. It is a place to indulge in pleasure and passion, to listen to music, watch films, converse, eat, drink, swim and, most importantly, to relax and enjoy the easily accessible markets and beaches on the southwest coast of Bali.

The entrance to the house is choreographed with immense skill. Located at the end of an unprepossessing narrow track perpendicular to Jalan Tegal Sari, nothing prepares the visitor for the magical spectacle that awaits. Arriving at a vehicle court in front of the house, a high transverse timber-clad wall blocks a view of the dwelling. A single vertical opening signals the entrance, and immediately beyond is a huge statue of Buddha. An outer courtyard with several frangipani trees and a second screen wall continue to delay views of the house until, finally, it is dramatically revealed.

The design is a striking U-shaped composition of planes, thin-edged slabs and slender concrete columns in the manner of the De Stijl or Gerrit Rietveld styles, arranged around a luminous blue swimming pool. Most of the external walls at ground level have been omitted to create open-sided naturally ventilated spaces suitable for living in the hot and humid tropics.

The house has two parallel wings linked by a roof terrace above a spacious dining area. The southern wing contains the living area, with a music center and DJ table overlooking the swimming pool. Above is the master bedroom suite, with extended eaves and shaded balconies. The northern wing contains the breakfast area, an indoor games area with a pool table, a sitting area and back-of-house activities, with a pitched shingle roof. Between the two wings is a central lawn, the linear swimming pool, which is the focus of the

Pages 110–11 The house is simultaneously simple yet strikingly beautiful.

Above A panoramic view of the house from the pool terrace.

house, and in the northeast corner of the garden a large video screen. A smaller shingle-roofed pavilion with sunken seating flanks the pool, and two additional bedrooms are located in a single-story pavilion at the eastern end of the garden beyond a timber pool deck. A vista to the east, of emerald green rice terraces and scenes of farmers in wide-brimmed hats, completes the idyllic setting.

There is a delightful convergence of traditional responses to climate, with a modern language of pristine white planar surfaces, voids, timber-clad boxes and slender columns. The influence of early Dutch modernism on the architecture is pervasive. Water is an essential element of the composition, which is thrown into sharp relief by the early morning and late afternoon sun.

The interior of the dwelling is by French interior designer Laure Deguillame, and the opportunity has been taken to integrate works of art with a collection of striking abstract paintings displayed on the white walls. Landscape design by Anton Clark complements the architecture.

Bali offers a taste of paradise to the many expatriates who visit the island, and Villa Kalyani is an exquisite jewel that embodies much of the appeal of the expatriate lifestyle.

Above The open-to-sky dining area and roof terrace.

Right The master bedroom suite hovers above the living area.

Above and left Two views of the open-sided living room—a wonderfully relaxed space.

Right A huge statue of Buddha is located at the entrance to the house.

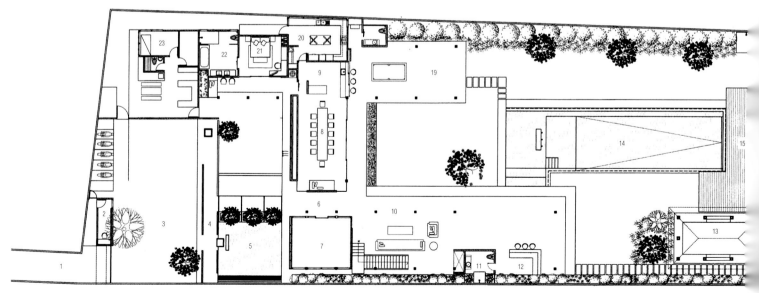

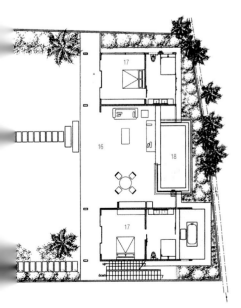

Opposite above Looking west at sunset over lush green paddy fields.

Left Ground floor plan.

Top A games area in the north wing.

Above A narrow horizontal opening gives a different framed view of the dining area and pool beyond.

0   5   10 meters

kayu aga house

CANGGU, BALI
ARCHITECT: YOKA SARA
BALE LEGEND ARCHITECT

Pages 120–1 The Kayu Aga house is a joyous eclectic celebratory dwelling.

Left The sensuous curve of the main living/dining accommodation.

Right A sculptural staircase con-structed from concrete, steel, timber and bamboo.

Yoka Sara is a Balinese architect who studied at the Architecture Department of Udayana University in Denpasar from 1983 to 1990. He credits Nyoman Gelebet, who taught in the school at that time, with giving him an understanding of the traditional architecture of Bali. At the same time, he says, "At that formative stage in my life, the book *Architecture: Form, Space & Order* by Francis D. K. Ching opened my eyes."[1] In 1989, he and two fellow students were commissioned to design the Balisani Hotel at Legian. The project launched his career and he curtailed his formal studies. They followed this up with the Balisani Suite at Batubelig, and in 1990 set up in practice as Kori D'Arch, a name that was changed two years later to PT Bale Legend.

The work of the practice expanded rapidly, and after par-ticipating in the design of Sekilak Island Resort, a private island at Batam (1992), and the Nikko Hotel at Sawangan (1994), the partners in the practice decided to expand into Design and Build. This venture into construction led to "a decline in the quality of our design and to a certain amount of repetition in our work," so in 1998 Yoka Sara decided to refocus on his original calling—to be a full-time design practice. The first commission of the rejuvenated practice was a house in Damansara Heights, Kuala Lumpur, followed by the Waka Gangga Resort (1999–2007) in collaboration with I Ketut Siandana, and further commissions that took the practice to Nagoya and Tokyo.

Yoka Sara's artistic flair is immediately apparent in the Kayu Aga House designed for Italian businessman Alberto Agazzi. The reasoning behind the plan form of the house is initially elusive. The compound essentially consists of a carport and three orthogonal sleeping pavilions located in the four corners of the site. Occupying the center is a two-story pavilion containing the principal living/dining facilities, with an elevated studio at first floor and a verdant roof garden. The central pavilion has a delightful oval staircase with bamboo balustrade rising from an elliptical pond. Each of the sleeping pavilions has a private garden court with a terrace and an outdoor bathroom, and the routes to the center are differently choreographed.

There appears to be an underlying rationale derived from a traditional Balinese compound, where family activities are assigned to different pavilions, but any resemblance to the traditional form is subverted by what at first seems a random arrangement of sinuous curved walls that serve to unify the various elements but simultaneously to separate the activities.

Yoka Sara's conceptual sketches provide insight into the design process and clarify the purpose of the walls. The site is divided into four layers from west to east, ex-pressed as slightly radiused lines, the first layer being a physical barrier to the noise from the road that runs along the western boundary. The barrier takes the form of a high wall and the service functions of the house tucked into the northeast corner of the site. The second layer is the "west lawn," that distances the main pavilion at the center of the plan from the noise source. The third layer is the linear structure of the central pavilion, with its elevated studio and roof garden, and the final layer, the "east lawn," between the central pavilion and the swimming pool. Notes in the margin of the architect's sketches dispel the notion that

the layering is random for there is a distinct hierarchy of privacy and formal zoning of uses.

Overlaid upon the west-to-east layers are more pronounced and flowing transverse curves that are expressed as free-standing walls. The walls diverge to frame views to the east over paddy fields and acknowledge the rising sun at dawn of each new day. These walls have a pattern of gray and green vertical stripes that is repeated on the entrance gate.

Finally, superimposed upon the system of lines is another system—one of movement. A processional route leads from the arrival court, in the southwest corner, in a northerly direction beneath a pergola to a point immediately west of the central pavilion, where a sharp turn to the east directs attention to a patio between the living and dining rooms, and thence to the east lawn. Notes in the margins of the architect's sketches describe this "journey" as a process of rejuvenation and discovery. Natural light is an important consideration in the genesis of the form, and some views are temporarily withheld by bamboo screens to arouse curiosity. The processional route extends to the 25-meter swimming pool with a gazebo, and beyond are tranquil views of rural life. A light wind blowing off the paddy fields stirs chiming bells.

The architectural language is totally modern and the design process is explained in terms of rational responses to site and climate, but ultimately the house is a visually delightful place with a myriad different moods and emotions. What more might one require of a home?

[1] Yoka Sara in e-mail correspondence with the author, February 2, 2010.

Above The east-facing façade of the house viewed from the swimming pool pavilion.

Opposite above left The processional route to the house beneath a cool shaded pergola.

Opposite above right A sleek kitchen/dining room is at the heart of the house.

Right The living area flows out to the east lawn.

Top The swimming pool pavilion.

Left and above Sinuous lines in the landscape.

Right Lines of sculptural columns unify the disparate elements of the plan.

Below Ground floor plan.

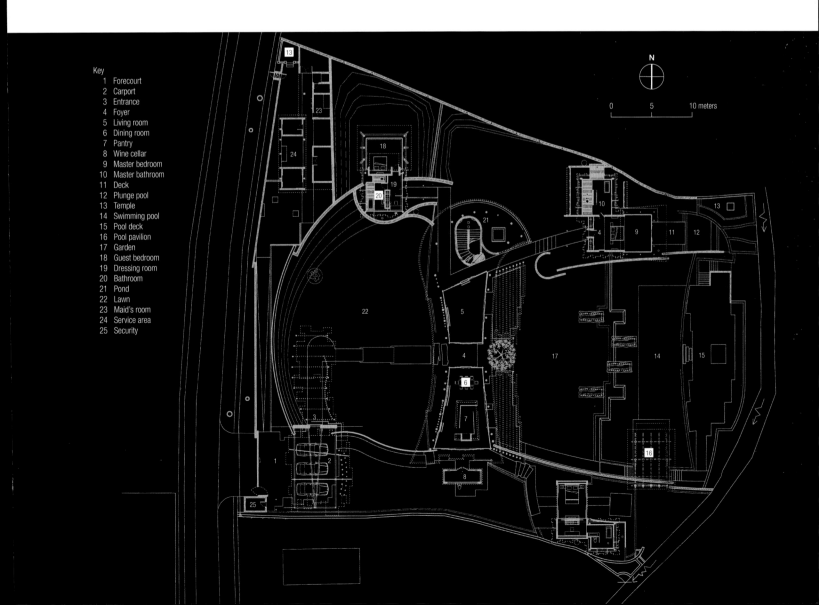

Key
1 Forecourt
2 Carport
3 Entrance
4 Foyer
5 Living room
6 Dining room
7 Pantry
8 Wine cellar
9 Master bedroom
10 Master bathroom
11 Deck
12 Plunge pool
13 Temple
14 Swimming pool
15 Pool deck
16 Pool pavilion
17 Garden
18 Guest bedroom
19 Dressing room
20 Bathroom
21 Pond
22 Lawn
23 Maid's room
24 Service area
25 Security

N

0   5   10 meters

Left The roof garden and studio overlook the west lawn.

Above The oval staircase with bamboo balusters punches through the curved roof of the central pavilion.

Right A pergola above the access route to a peripheral sleeping pavilion.

Far right The east lawn.

rumah kemang

JAKARTA
ARCHITECT: YORI ANTAR
HAN AWAL & PARTNERS ARCHITECTS

Yori Antar was born in Jakarta in 1962, the son of the widely respected architect Han Awal. He studied architecture at the University of Indonesia and graduated in 1989. Imbued with a deep concern for conservation and the natural world acquired from his father, Yori Antar was an activist during his student days and a leading figure in the formation of Arsitek Muda Indonesia (AMI). Yori's father worked with Y. B. Mangunwijaya on projects such as a church in Cilincing, North Jakarta, so that Yori grew up with a deep respect for the work of Roma Mangun, as Mangunwijaya was popularly known. "He was a genius," Yori says. "He took the knowledge he obtained in Germany, and when he began designing buildings in Indonesia, he integrated modernity with local materials and values."[1]

In the early 1990s, Yori Antar was among those breaking the boundaries of the profession, collaborating with

artists, anthropologists and sociologists to learn from people living in traditional settlements and houses.[2] Today, one of the leading designers of his generation, he is still involved in activities that seek to protect and revitalize traditional communities and their way of life. "I'm not saying I've become a traditional architect. I'm still a modern-day architect, but one who wants to try to appreciate our own roots," he points out. And so, under the Rumah Asuh project initiated by his practice, Yori takes young architects and architecture students to remote villages where traditional communities struggle to survive. Supported by funding from the Tirto Foundation, he helps locals rebuild and renovate their homes. "Traditional houses of the Waerebo in Flores and Lesser Sunda," he says, "are made from locally sourced materials that are put together in a structure that forms the perfect shelter. Young architects today can learn from

these structures. There are joint details that can be applied to modern structures."

How, then, are we to connect this knowledge to dwellings for the urban middle and upper middle classes? The client, the proprietor of the Bluebird taxi firm, had traveled widely and studied overseas, so that many ideas, some unpredictable, were brought to the brief and the design was the outcome of a continuous dialog.

Rumah Kemang is a spectacular house comprising four interconnected pavilions arranged around a courtyard. Unusually, the house has two entrances: a formal modern portico and a traditional Balinese-inspired gateway. Both are accessed from the short entrance drive.

The formal entrance is the principal route into the house, the Balinese gateway being reserved for festival occasions as it leads, via a path round the side of the house, to a thatch-roofed garden pavilion at the end of a 25-meter swimming pool. There is a distinct hierarchy of privacy in the

Pages 130–1 The veranda is a wonderful space in the early evening.

Above The broad veranda outside the living area overlooks a lush green garden surrounded by mature trees.

Right The focus of the garden is a sparkling ultramarine pool and a thatch-roofed pavilion.

dwelling. Alongside the entrance portico is a waiting area, not unlike a Malay *serambi*, where casual visitors can be received outside the home. Invited to enter through a wide teak door, a rectangular "Javanese" courtyard encircled by a veranda gives access to a guest suite and the public rooms of the house, namely the living room and the dining room. At the center of the courtyard is a frangipani tree surrounded by a pond fed by a bubbling fountain.

A glazed lobby connects the living room to the most private accommodation, which includes three children's rooms and a family area linked to a broad terrace overlooking the rear garden and the "borrowed landscape" of mature trees beyond the site boundary. Above the children's rooms is the "kids' domain," an attic accessed by steep stairs from each of the children's rooms. This is the only two-story part of the dwelling. At the rear of the house is the master bedroom suite, with an exclusive semicircular walled courtyard.

A large entourage of staff, with the duties of maid, cook, driver, gardener and security guard, are located in quarters at the front of the house to provide surveillance.

There are numerous works of art—a painting by Suprobo, sculptural works by F. Widayanto and Teguh Ostenrik, and a petrified tree from Antique Bali Gallery—incorporated into the design, along with Yori Antar's trademark—textures and louvered screens incorporating local materials.

[1] Yori Antar in conversation with the author, October 23, 2009.
[2] Anissa S. Febrina, "Learning from Genius Loci," *Jakarta Post*, January 11, 2010.

Key

1	Forecourt	16	Pantry
2	Carport	17	Wet kitchen
3	Security	18	Storeroom
4	Driver's sitting area	19	Maid's bedroom
5	Terrace	20	Maid's living room
6	Entrance foyer	21	Library
7	Garage	22	Bedroom
8	Reflecting pool	23	Master bedroom
9	Guest living area	24	Wardrobe
10	Guest bedroom	25	Master bathroom
11	Veranda	26	Swimming pool
12	Fish pond	27	Garden
13	Lotus pond	28	Gazebo
14	Living room	29	Dog's cage
15	Dining room	30	Pool changing room

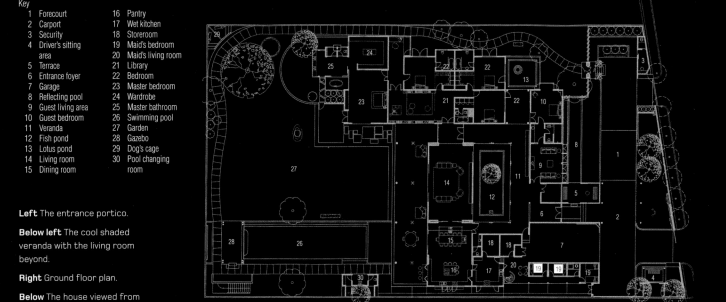

Left The entrance portico.

Below left The cool shaded veranda with the living room beyond.

Right Ground floor plan.

Below The house viewed from the garden at dusk.

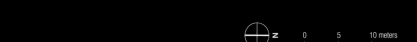

0   5   10 meters

sunrise house

JAKARTA
ARCHITECT: KUSUMA AGUSTIANTO
KUSAMA AGUSTIANTO ARCHITECT

Kusuma Agustianto was born in Purwokerto, Central Java, in 1971, and received his architectural education at Parahyangan Catholic University in Bandung, where he graduated in 1995. In the same year, he won first prize in a competition for the design of Bandung Railway Station that brought him to the attention of his contemporaries. He joined the established architectural practice of Graha-cipta Hadiprana, where he worked on the design of residences in Jakarta, Bandung and Bali. He resigned to set up his own practice, Kusuma Agustianto Architect, in 2005, and has focused on private residences, villas and offices in Jakarta, Semarang, Magelang, Surabaya and Bali.

During the period from 1997 to 1999, Agustianto traveled extensively with the Arsitek Muda Indonesia group to gain knowledge of the architecture of Singapore, Malaysia, Thailand and Australia, but a 2000 architectural tour to Japan was particularly inspiring, and the quality of the finishes in his house designs are evidence of this.

The Sunrise House is located on the edge of a small green square, a public park, where local people cultivate bananas. A typical Jakarta urban house form on a rectangular site, the dwelling is enclosed on three sides by high walls; it is surprising how many variations are possible employing this simple urban typology, with its intricate separation of front-of-house and back-of-house activities. There are no distant views from the house—no long vistas—so that the life of the house is concentrated intensely on the interior. Two deep internal courtyards and a front garden court give solar shading and promote air movement. In many ways, the typology is similar to that of Sri Lanka, possibly as a result of a shared Dutch influence on urban planning.

The first impression of the Sunrise House is of meticulous attention to detail, initially displayed in the design of the entrance gate and the copper-colored carved timber entrance door. The house is entered in the north corner of the site, whereupon a sharp turn left leads into a small courtyard with a *koi* pond. On encountering a timber-floored terrace, shoes are removed before entering a wide lobby with a guest bedroom to the left overlooking a lushly landscaped garden. Beyond the guest suite is a central

Pages 138–9 The house has a simple understated entrance.

Right The living room is well ventilated and benefits from daylight provided by two courtyards.

Key
5 Guest bedroom
10 Master bedroom
11 Study room
12 Gallery
13 Wardrobe
14 Bathroom
15 Bathroom
16 Maid's room
17 Services
18 Roof garden

Opposite above left Light enters the house through a delicately detailed pergola.

Opposite above right The living room viewed over a shallow pool.

Opposite below First floor plan.

Left The house demonstrates perfectly the advantages of building around courtyards in the tropics.

Above The public façade of the house gives no hint of the light and openness within.

square courtyard with a pond. The living/dining space lies beyond this courtyard, along with a Western-style fitted kitchen. Beyond and on axis is the rear courtyard, enhanced by a splendid frangipani tree.

The upper floors of the house are also orientated inward to the rear courtyard and central courtyard, while two smaller bedrooms are orientated toward the front garden. At the summit of the house is a roof terrace for parties.

The architect has mastered the art of interlocking space. The house is reminiscent of a Rubik cube, with a strictly orthogonal relationship of interconnecting solids and voids. The route through the house is via a series of axial

movements. Top-lit courtyards allow daylight to penetrate to the core of the house. The deep courtyards provide shading from the morning and evening sun and promote air movement.

The Sunrise House, designed in collaboration with Mega Sarana, Yandi Prayudhi and Lignet Roset for entrepreneur Saksono Banyuaji and his family, is a beautiful object, like a jewel—sparingly fashioned without excess or waste, producing a sharp blend of urban chic and sophistication. The finishes are of exceptionally high quality, with floors of white marble and bleached timber and a ceiling with a basket weave finish.

Left The design exhibits masterly use of interlocking space.

Top left, center and right Sunlight enters the house, casting a myriad different entrancing patterns.

Above View to an internal court.

CANGGU, BALI
ARCHITECT: POPO DANES
POPO DANES ARCHITECT

villa
ombak luwung

Popo Danes, who was born in Banyuwatis in north Bali in 1964, studied at the Architecture Department, Udayana University at Denpasar, where he graduated in 1991. Danes has not strayed far from his roots, designing in a manner that makes a direct connection with the traditional architecture of the island. One of his mentors was the respected architect and academic Robi Sularto Sastrowardoyo, but he was also inspired as a young architect by the work of Frank Lloyd Wright, Eero Saarinan and Kenzo Tange. In 1992, with a scholarship from Rotary International, Danes traveled to the Netherlands on a group study exchange, where he immersed himself in European modernism during trips to design studios, museums and building sites. In 1993, he established his own architectural design firm, Popo Danes Architect.

Located at Canggu, an upmarket resort area north of Kuta, on the west coast of Bali overlooking the Indian Ocean, Villa Ombak Luwung is entered through an elegant sliding gate in the northeast corner of the site. A grass thatch *alang-alang* roofed pavilion faces into the vehicle court, which has space for four cars parked in pairs on either side of the entrance archway. Accommodation for domestic staff is in the upper story of the pavilion. Proceeding beneath the arched entrance, an axis leads in a northwest direction, beneath a pergola bedecked with flowering plants and alongside a rectangular pond strewn with lilies, to arrive at a raised circular fountain. The axis continues beyond the fountain to terminate at a gigantic carved stone sculpture, but the fountain itself marks the fulcrum of the plan from which a second, perpendicular axis leads northeast to a "media" pavilion, which contains a first-floor guest suite, and southwest to the private domain of the villa.

Taking the southwest axis and penetrating through a heavily sculptured transverse stone wall with a narrow opening in the form of a traditional gateway, a number of pavilions devoted to distinct functions are arranged around an elevated central, double-roofed entertainment space, perhaps inspired by a village *Bale Agung* or assembly hall. To the south is the master bedroom suite, with a palatial bathroom, and to the west and northwest of the central pavilion two more pavilions housing more bedrooms and a

Pages 146–7 The beachfront house in Bali combines the artistic skills of architect Popo Danes and landscape designer Bill Bensley.

Above The design embodies many aspects of Balinese culture and tradition.

Right Section through the site.

Key
4 Media room
5 Living area
14 Courtyard
16 Swimming pool
18 Fountain
19 Bedroom 3

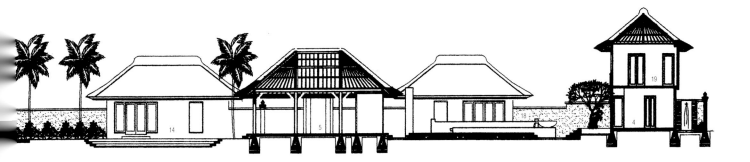

Left The entrance to the house beneath a magical flower-bedecked pergola.

Right A sunken grass court is located on the central axis.

Below right A raised circular stone fountain marks the inter-section of the entrance path and the central axis.

luxury spa/massage space. Further to the southwest, the axis continues across a sunken grass court and then over a raised outdoor chessboard, eventually arriving at an infinity pool. Beyond is a palm-fringed beach and the Indian Ocean. A traditional *lumbung* rice barn provides a quiet refuge overlooking the breaking waves, and two fishing boats are drawn up on the shoreline.

Like the traditional Balinese residential compound, the different functions of the household are carried out in separate pavilions. The elements of the plan follow an underlying orthogonal grid that unifies the composition and is suggestive of the nine-square mandala that determines the organization of a traditional Balinese family compound. It is overlaid by the distinctly modernist notion of progressing through space in a series of framed axial movements, culminating in vistas or objects in the landscape. A sophisticated interpretation of a traditional Balinese compound, the house is the romantic vacation home of Ryan Padgett, a Singapore-based businessman, and his wife Teresa. Landscaping commissioned by the couple and designed by the Bangkok-based landscape architect Bill Bensley complements perfectly the architecture of Popo Danes.

Inevitably, the question arises: Is the residence "new" in the sense that most of the dwellings in this book use a contemporary architectural language. Other questions follow: Is it simply a reuse of tradition? Is it renewing tradition? Adapting tradition? Transforming tradition? It is evident that Danes is keenly aware of the paradoxes of building in a traditional style for a modern world. In 2002, his work was published under the title *Bali: Living in Two Worlds—A Critical Self Portrait*, that recognizes the duality

in his work.[1] It is also evident that he regards his work as a "transformation," for this was the theme of an exhibition of his work in 2004.[2]

Although he is a product of the modern cultural blend that is contemporary Bali, Popo has not lost touch with his heritage. He still retains something of the *undagi*, the traditional Balinese architect who works to balance the house with its natural surroundings and with its inhabitants. It can be argued, too, that tradition is not static and the design insures that Balinese forms of construction and the technical skills of local artisans are not lost. Ultimately, this "contemporary vernacular"[3] house is a sublime retreat, providing an opportunity for rest and contemplation.

[1] Popo Danes, *Bali: Living in Two Worlds—A Critical Self Portrait*, Basel: Derkulturen Museum, 2002.

[2] Popo Danes, *Transformation: Solo Exhibition of Architecture*, Denpasar, Bali, February 7–15, 2004.

[3] William S. W. Lim and Tan Hock Beng, *Contemporary Vernacular: Evoking Traditions in Asian Architecture*, Singapore: Select Books, 1998.

Opposite above left A small pavilion is devoted to a luxury spa/massage space.

Opposite above right Another pavilion houses the master bedroom.

Opposite below and above A tall living space inspired by the traditional *Bale Agung* is at the very heart of the plan.

Below Ground floor plan.

Key
1 Carpark
2 Garage/carport
3 Entrance
4 Media room
5 Living room
6 Dining room
7 Kitchen
8 Master bedroom
9 Master bathroom
10 Bedroom 1
11 Bedroom 2
12 Bathroom
13 Spa
14 Countyard
15 Pool deck
16 Swimming pool
17 Pond
18 Fountain

Above The central axis culminates at an infinity pool and beyond is the Indian Ocean.

Left The swimming pool deck.

Right Access to guest accommodation located above the media room is via an external stair.

ampera house

JAKARTA
ARCHITECTS: GREGORIUS SUPIE YOLODI & MARIA ROSANTINA
D-ASSOCIATES

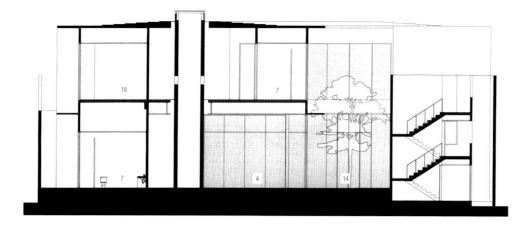

Key
4   Gallery
7   Bathroom
14 Garden court
19 Dressing room

Pages 156–7 The home of one of Indonesia's top fashion designers is entered through a transparent glass box.

Left Section drawing.

Right and far right The processional route from the entrance via the lobby.

Below The reception room/gallery opens out to a secluded courtyard.

Gregorius Supie Yolodi was born in Jakarta in 1974 and studied architecture at the Parahyangan Catholic University in Bandung. Upon graduation in 1998, he found employment in a variety of roles and in a number of architectural firms, including Grahacipta Hadiprana, prior to forming his own practice, d-associates, in 2000. His Km19 Project, the first gas station and rest area on a toll road in Indonesia, won an Isatan Arsitek Indonesia Award in 2009. His business partner, Maria Rosantina, is also a 1998 graduate of Parahyangan Catholic University, who joined d-associates in 2002 after working with several firms, including PT Rekamatra.

Asked to name designers who have influenced his work, Yolodi expresses admiration for the work of Le Corbusier and also, at a much smaller scale, for the sensitive projects of the Yogyakarta-based architect Eko Agus Prawoto. He admits Louis Kahn also influenced his approach to design, and he also admires the work of Geoffrey Bawa, which he saw on a visit to Sri Lanka in 2009.

This appreciation of designs at opposite ends of the architectural spectrum is reflected in the Ampera House, that is both a home and a gallery for a client who works in the fashion industry and whose gorgeously elegant creations have been a mainstay on the Indonesian social scene for the past two decades.

"Notwithstanding his highly publicized life in the fashion world, the owner is a very private man when not at work. The house is consequently hidden behind a screen of mature trees, and semi-mature trees were planted at the rear of the plot two years ago to insure privacy," says Yolodi.[1] "The emphasis is on quietness, silence and retreat from the city. Nothing was to be visible from the outside as the client wished to separate his private life from his public persona."

A processional route gently ascends from the arrival court to the entrance lobby in a series of axial shifts, via a ramp and through a gap in a screen wall, to a guest reception pavilion in the form of a glass box, and thence to a lobby

leading to an art gallery. A large sliding door separates the arrival court and an inner courtyard. The client has a passionate interest in modern Indonesian painting, and the gallery is designed to showcase his collection, which includes large paintings by Waka, Made Jirna and Harris Purnomo. One wall of the gallery opens out to a landscaped courtyard with a "green wall," separating what Louis Kahn defined as the "served" and "servant" spaces in a dwelling.

But the most significant feature of the Ampera House is the voluminous living/dining area. The client required a large space "framing" the enclosed garden and swimming pool beyond. In sharp contrast to this spacious light-filled double-height rectangular volume is a long gentle stair-case compressed between two vertical planes beneath a continuous roof light, that facilitates access from the ground floor living area to the first floor rooms.

The living room and art gallery occupy the center of the plan, effectively linking two wings, one accommodating private activities, including bedrooms, bathrooms and a gym; the other essentially housing the back-of-house activities of the dwelling: kitchens, garage, maid's rooms, storage, plant room and laundry.

The house owner has a large extended family who visit frequently, and thus the five bedrooms are each fitted with an *en suite* bathroom. The owner also has a number of dogs that are, he says, "like family to me." They are housed in a separate annex in a corner of the rear garden.

Yolodi manipulates space with great dexterity, juxtaposing large light-filled volumes with narrow compressed routes, and in the process creates a series of stimulating and pleasurable spatial experiences.

[1] Gregorius Supie Yolodi in conversation with the author, February 12, 2010.

Above View from the first-floor gallery to the dining/living room and the pool beyond.

Left Tall glazed doors facing the rear courtyard open to permit natural ventilation and create scintillating shadows.

Left The living/dining room is an awesome space.

Right The first-floor access corridor.

Far right The compressed space of the principal staircase sharply contrasts with the openness of the living/dining area.

Below An upper gallery gives access to the principal bedrooms.

Key
1	Car porch	7	Bathroom	13	Garage	19	Dressing room
2	Entrance	8	Gym	14	Garden court	20	Services
3	Guest reception	9	Storeroom	15	Pond	21	Laundry
4	Gallery	10	Pantry	16	Swimming pool	22	Drying area
5	Living room	11	Kitchen	17	Library	23	Dog kennels
6	Bedroom	12	Maid's room	18	Sitting room		

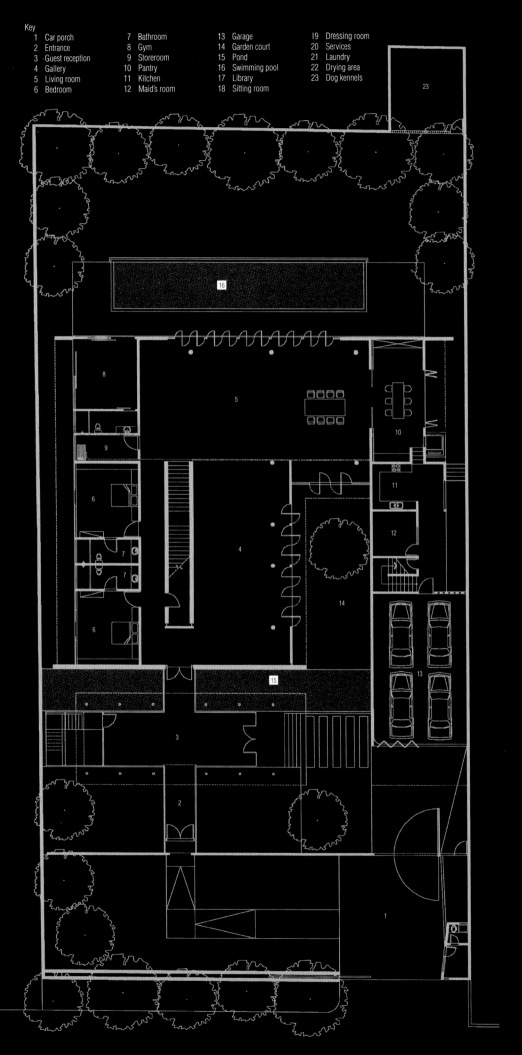

Opposite The expansive scale of the house is apparent from the swimming pool courtyard.

Left Ground floor plan.

Above The dining area viewed from the gallery.

Below Detail of the stairwell.

0   5   10 meters

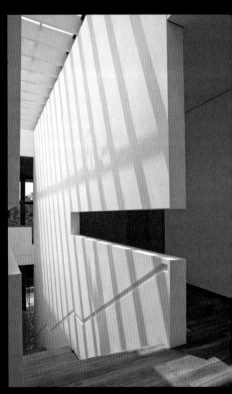

villa dewi sri

TIBUBENENG, BALI
ARCHITECT: WALTER WAGNER
HABITAT 5

Walter Wagner is a native of Landsberg am Lech in southwest Bavaria, Germany. Born in 1959, he graduated from the Fachhochscule in Munich in 1987. In 1991, he became a Member of the Bavarian Institute of Architects and set up practice with Robert Gießl under the name ARcTEC. Between 1991 and 1997, he designed a number of projects in Indonesia and Australia, and in 2000 formed a new practice, Habitat 5, based in Kuta on the island of Bali.

Villa Dewi Sri is a vacation home located northwest of Denpasar, the capital of the province of Bali and the principal point of entry to the island by air. The dwelling occupies a 20 m wide x 75 m long plot that once formed an agricultural holding. The house is entered from a vehicle court and carport shared with an adjoining villa, through a ceremonial gateway set into a high wall. The route then follows a curved path across stepping stones through an attractive water garden to a linear gallery on the central axis of the site. The gallery is flanked by two suites, each containing a double bedroom, a palatial bathroom and the ubiquitous outdoor bathing facilities that insure the complete Bali experience. The two suites are accessed from a shaded veranda that is placed transversely across the central axis, with a staircase that gives access to a third suite of rooms at first-floor level, with two double bedrooms, en suite bathrooms and a wide balcony with access to a roof garden.

The central axis continues down a shallow flight of stairs to a timber pool deck and a 25-meter lap pool. Arranged along one side of the garden are an open-sided kitchen, a breakfast room, dining room and living room, culminating in a veranda with views east over paddy fields. The rooms can be closed by means of sliding glazed doors.

The defining feature of the house, that sets it apart from many others, is the extensive roof garden above the living and dining areas. The roof insulates the rooms below and insures that the greenery removed by the very act of building is partially replaced, thus encouraging biodiversity.

Pages 166–7 Daily activities take place in the open-sided living room overlooking the pool.

Opposite The entrance lobby and veranda.

Top There are magnificent views from the pool terrace toward lush green rice terraces.

Above The processional route from the carport to the entrance lobby via a water garden.

Below A detail of the roof planting box.

Bottom The living room with its sustainable insulated "green roof."

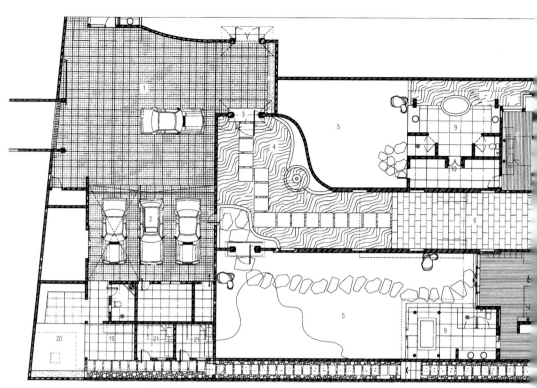

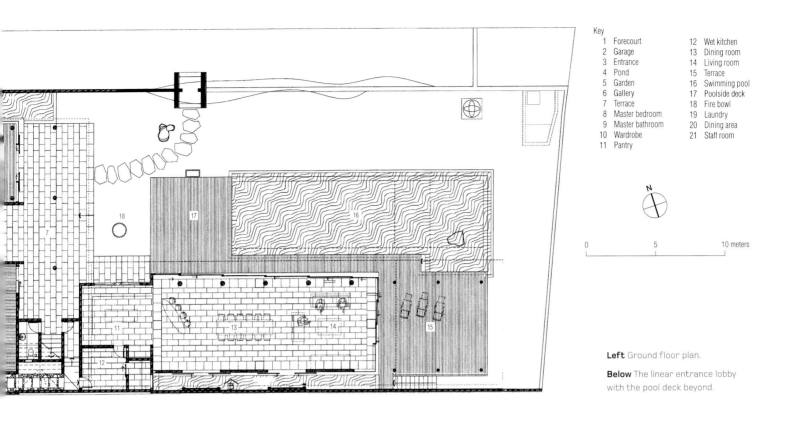

Key
1	Forecourt	12	Wet kitchen
2	Garage	13	Dining room
3	Entrance	14	Living room
4	Pond	15	Terrace
5	Garden	16	Swimming pool
6	Gallery	17	Poolside deck
7	Terrace	18	Fire bowl
8	Master bedroom	19	Laundry
9	Master bathroom	20	Dining area
10	Wardrobe	21	Staff room
11	Pantry		

Left Ground floor plan.

Below The linear entrance lobby with the pool deck beyond.

tulodong
bawah house

JAKARTA
ARCHITECT: DENNY GONDOJATMIKO
DENNY GONDO ARCHITECT

Denny Gondojatmiko was born in Parwokerto in 1969 and studied architecture at Parahyangan Catholic University in Bandung. A contemporary of Tan Tik Lam and Ahmad Djuhara, he graduated in 1994, after which he worked for Ciputra for five years and then with Jeffrey Budiman Architects before setting up Denny Gondo Architects in 2004. He has, in a relatively short time, built up a considerable reputation as a designer of exquisite modern residences. He is a committed member of Arsitek Muda Indonesia and has traveled to Europe and Japan with the group. The architect has designed a number of houses, including several high-quality residences in the Lippo Karawachi development. His work has appeared in *The Phaidon Atlas of 21st Century World Architecture* (2008).

The Tulodong Bawah House is the home of the manufacturer and exporter of Natural Habitat furniture, which has production facilities in Central Java. Conceptually, the house is a simple box elevated above the street, for at the outset the decision was taken to raise the living spaces and insert a garage at ground level. This reduced the amount of expensive excavation of a basement and gave views out over the street from the principal living areas. This visual connection with the neighborhood reverses a trend in urban residential design in Jakarta to turn inward and present

a blank façade to the street. It became apparent at the planning stage that it would also be possible to insert an office at ground level, thereby cutting down on the journey to work and making the house much more sustainable.

The most visible feature of the house is a vertical "green wall" that links to a planted garden at first-floor level, which is then connected to a second-floor garden. The green wall gives the house a distinctive appearance in the neighborhood and makes a substantial contribution to retaining biodiversity.

The house is entered from Jalan Tulodong Bawah via a lobby that is slightly off-center and serves both the private dwelling and the office. A straight flight of steps leads directly to the center of the open-plan house, where a tall deep-grained timber door gives direct access to the kitchen/pantry, dining room, living room and an external timber deck. In a composition that is generally resolved in shades of gray and brown, there is a splash of Van Gogh sunflower yellow in the kitchen. A lap pool occupies the full width of the rear courtyard, with a raised planter and a fountain concealing a corner lightwell that introduces daylight and ventilation into the maidspace below. The sound of water pervades the house and light floods into the living spaces through the full-height glazed sliding

Pages 172–3 The entrance façade of the house incorporates extensive vegetation.

Left The living area opens onto a glittering blue lap pool.

Right and far right Filtered sunlight illuminates the principal staircase and upper floor spaces.

Below Section drawing.

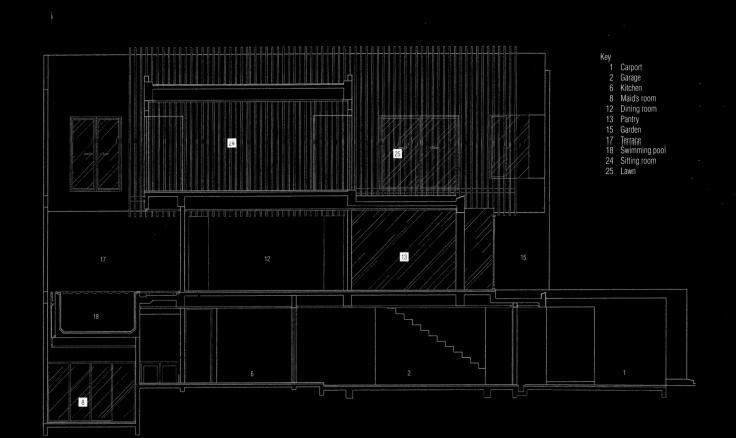

Key
1 Carport
2 Garage
6 Kitchen
8 Maid's room
12 Dining room
13 Pantry
15 Garden
17 Terrace
18 Swimming pool
24 Sitting room
25 Lawn

Above A glass-bottomed *koi* pond is located above the entrance to the house.

Left A window seat offers views at treetop level.

Below The living room veranda has extensive views over the street.

doors that face the courtyard. The first floor of the house, where the architect utilizes butt-jointed glass, is strikingly transparent.

Directly ahead, on axis, is a flight of stairs to the upper floor containing the master bedroom suite, a child's room projecting over the pool and a bathroom. The accommodation is completed with a family room and a *koi* pond located over the house entrance. A steep external flight of stairs ascends to a roof deck.

There is a strong sense of De Stijl-like order in the modernist vocabulary and an excellent resolution of tectonics. Cruciform steel columns, that make reference to Mies van der Rohe's Barcelona Pavilion, are utilized to support the master bedroom suite above the living room deck. Gondo expresses his admiration of the work of Tan Tjiang Ay, a doyen of the architectural profession in Indonesia, who has maintained a steady and uncompromising output of modern architecture. He also expresses admiration for the work of American architect Peter Bohlin of Bohlin Cywinski Jackson (Arcadian Architecture), who successfully combines wood and steel in his designs, and the influence of both architects can be detected in Gondo's design.

This is an elegant design replete with ideas on sustainability, daylight and natural ventilation. The essence of the house is in its compactness, tactile surfaces and transparency—and vertical gardens that replace greenery lost at ground level.

Above The house is an elegantly composed cubist form.

Right View of a passing street hawker from the roof terrace.

villa at
alila soori

KLATING, BALI
ARCHITECT: CHAN SOO KHIAN
SCDA ARCHITECTS

Born and raised in Penang, Chan Soo Khian undertook his architectural education at Washington University and Yale University. Against a backdrop of diverse design philosophies at Yale University School of Art and Architecture, Chan set out to ground himself in classicism. The classical language of architecture significantly influenced his development as an architect. It was a focus from which he went on to appreciate the works of the modern masters. Chan worked as an intern with Kohn Pederson Fox before returning to Asia, where he joined A61 Architects in Singapore, leaving to set up his own design studio in 1995. Two years later, he established SCDA Architects. The practice has subsequently established a reputation for designing buildings that explore a modern language rooted in the Southeast Asian context.

In 2006, Chan and his Indonesian fiancée Ling were looking for a site to build a vacation home in Bali. They chanced upon a beautiful location at Klating in the Tabanan Regency, with stunning sunsets over the Indian Ocean, rice terraces stepping down to the beach, a cave, a waterfall and a temple on a headland to the north. After many months of negotiation with the elders of the local *banjar*, they acquired the site along with a right of access through the nearby village, but by then their plans had changed. Building one house simply did not "stack up" financially, so they decided to build a resort of 48 dwellings varying in size from one bedroom to ten bedrooms and including eight three-bedroom villas. In February 2007, Chan commenced the design of what turned out to be a small village, with a capacity for 164 guests and 180 permanent staff and numerous casual workers.

Chan's intentions were "to design employing a contemporary vernacular architectural language and to create a comfortable, energy-efficient resort style of living that mostly uses natural ventilation."[1] Recycled sewage water is treated and used for landscape irrigation. The flat roofs are covered with porous volcanic stones that are good insulators for heat. *Sukabumi* stone and the light gray volcanic *Paras Kelating* that are used for cladding are locally sourced, and terracotta, which is a craft available in the nearby village, is used extensively in the design. The site planning builds upon the natural terrain and blends into the rice field and black sand beach.

In October 2009, as I accompanied Chan through the narrow main street, he remarked that "It was always my dream to build a piece of paradise such as this and to work 'hands on' with the local workmen and see the project realized." In March 2010, the resort was launched as Alila Soori.

The villa illustrated here is not a house in the sense that it functions solely as a single family home but it is true of many vacation dwellings in Bali that are rented to visitors and friends. The three-bedroom residence is entered from the village street through a tall timber door and thence via a flight of external steps to a veranda. Looking east from the entrance there is a splendid bucolic landscape with maize

Pages 178–9 Alila Soori is an enchanting holiday village with a variety of vacation villas.

Above Perimeter stone walls protect the exclusiveness of each villa.

Opposite The entrance stairs ascend to the first-floor lobby.

fields, rice terraces and grazing cattle. An inner door leads to the entrance lobby and from there to the pool deck and a pool pavilion with an entrancing view to the west over the crescent-shaped bay and the temple on the headland. One's instinct is to breath a deep sigh of contentment, slow down, stop and simply watch the mesmerising breakers roll in from the ocean and spill onto the beach.

The architecture of the dwelling utilizes all the tactics that Chan has perfected in an extensive oeuvre of residential designs—a lucid modern language and a choreographed route through the house—with white terrazzo walls, timber screens, soft silk fabrics, reflective pools and carefully orchestrated vistas. In addition to this, Chan's uncompromising attention to detail is evident in the placing of artifacts, the junctions of materials and the custom-designed furniture.

In 2002, Chan received the Architecture Review (UK) Merit Award for Emerging Architecture, an award that confirmed his growing international reputation, a judgment endorsed by the selection of SCDA by Architectural Record (USA) as one of their Year 2003 Design Vanguard firms. In 2006, he was presented with the Singapore Institute of Architects—Getz Architecture Prize for Emergent Architecture in Asia and later, in 2006, the quality of his work was recognized with the inaugural Singapore President's Design Award.

[1] Chan Soo Khian in conversation with the author, October 28, 2009.

Above The pool pavilion.

Opposite above and below
The living area looks out to
the glittering blue pool.

Opposite center A luxury
bathroom suite.

Key
1 Entrance
2 Lobby
3 Living room
4 Master bedroom
5 Master bathroom
6 Walk-in closet
7 Bedroom
8 Bathroom
9 Lawn
10 Deck
11 Swimming pool
12 Pavilion
13 Void
14 Pantry

0   5   10 meters

Above The vacation villa looks west and the residents enjoy stunning sunsets over the Indian Ocean.

Below The entrance to the house is through a tall timber door opening onto the "village" street.

sunaryo house

BANDUNG
DESIGNER: SUNARYO
SELASAR SUNARYO ART SPACE

Pages 186–7 The artist's house is embraced by the landscape.

Left The artist at work in his studio.

Right The house enjoys natural ventilation.

Far right A splash of red highlights the principal structural roof member of the garden pavilion.

Below The broad veranda outside the artist's studio where his recently completed works await collection

Sunaryo, one of Indonesia's most eminent artists, came to the conclusion in 2008 that he required a new painting studio, whereupon he decided to build a studio with a small living space on a steep hillside site he owned at Meta Wangi, north of Bandung.[1] He had earlier reconstructed a traditional Javanese timber dwelling acquired in Solo on the upper part of the site, alongside the entrance, with the intention of providing accommodation for visiting artists and performers at Selasar Sunaryo Art Space, the nearby art center, which is now visited by an average of 30,000 people every year.

By the beginning of 2009, Sunaryo's new studio project was "on site" and the artist, armed with his own sketches, was personally supervising the construction. In a little over one year, it was complete. The accommodation is minimal. A large painting studio, the *raison d'être* of the project, is located in the sub-basement, with a covered outdoor veranda and courtyard accessed by a ramp from the site entrance to facilitate the arrival and removal of Sunaryo's canvases.

The entrance to the living accommodation is a processional route from the main gate, traversing the hillside along a path of large flat stones and timber balks set in grass, with glimpses of the building withheld until it is finally revealed. The living accommodation consists of a simple bedroom and a small breakfast room with attached kitchen, accessed directly from a spacious living space. A bathroom and a guest reception space with a daybed are located at the rear of the house. The focus of the living room is a huge table hewn from the trunk of a single large tree, capable of seating sixteen people, and set in a sunken pit with fixed seating around it. The table is just one of a several places around the house for groups of family, visiting artists or friends to gather. Each sitting area has a different perspective: the guest reception space overlooks a *koi* pond and is a quiet place for reflection; a veranda outside the living room gives a view over verdant green agricultural terraces to the south, and there is a bench where visitors can remove their shoes before entering the house.

At the lower level, reached by an external staircase along-side a tiny waterfall, there is a thatch-roofed pavilion and two more external sitting places, each offering a different place to contemplate nature and the activities of farmers on the opposite side of the valley. The artist speaks of "my small house" with immense pleasure and tells a story, no doubt apocryphal, of how he built it without informing his wife, and when she asked where he was going each day, he replied, "I am just going down to the garden." He explains that he wanted to construct a place of silence for painting and contemplation. In the event, he suffered a heart attack when the house was half complete, and upon his recovery his doctor advised he swim every day. The result was that a swimming pool was added at the end of the lower terrace.

The design is an inscription on the 1.6-ha site, a work of art

in the landscape. Sunaryo is a genius, and there is magic in everything he produces. Below the house is an extensive terraced garden with rows of vegetables and fruit. He has also planted 1,000 trees. There are splashes of red that highlight certain details—a device he often employs in his paintings. Here, the sudden appearance of red can be found in a handrail or a roofing member or the smooth infill of resin in a knot in the timber dining table. Even the artist's spectacles have red frames!

In the design and construction of the house, there is a direct connection between the end user and the designer through the artisans who constructed the house using simple technology and the skills available to most builders of kampong houses. Sunaryo did the drawings for the house on scraps of paper, canvas or cardboard that were to

hand. Sunaryo's neighbors, in the spirit of *gotong-royong*, constructed the house, although he is quick to point out that he optimized the abilities of everyone who offered to help—and he paid for their assistance but not excessively so that money was spent in an economical way. This immediacy is evident and contrasts sharply with industrial practices of house construction where the end user might be five steps removed from the contractor, with an intermediary role being played by the architect, the architectural assistant, the contractor and the craftsman.

The house is constructed with what, at first, seem permeable bamboo walls except that, because he feels the cold in Bandung, Sunaryo has inserted an insulating leaf of brick between the inner and outer layers of woven bamboo screens, and the openings in the external wall can be closed with frameless glass windows. Elsewhere he employs a variety of tactile materials: rough-hewn timber, concrete with exposed aggregate and plaited bamboo.

Sunaryo has a creative family. His wife Heti Komalasari is a skilled artist in her own right, being much in demand for traditional Sumbanese wedding makeup and sometimes traveling abroad to organize the wedding preparations for Indonesian diasporas. His daughter Mita, a fashion designer, works with Liz Claibourne in New York, and one of his sons, Arin, studied at St Martins College of Art London and two of his paintings are hung in the living area.

Above left The focus of the living area is a huge sunken table hewn from a single tree.

Above The pedestrian entrance to the house via an external veranda. Each sitting area gives a different perspective.

Ultimately, the studio and accompanying living space is not architecture with a capital A but together with the garden it is essentially an "art installation" resulting from a spatial strategy comprising lines, objects, focal points and vistas. This ability to "play with space, objects and forms" is acknowledged as one of Sunaryo's great skills, and here he transfers the techniques that are evident in his paintings onto a larger canvas without borders.[2] The internal spaces and the framing of views in and out of the house are thrilling, and there are lessons that all architects can learn from the relationship of the building to the landscape.

[1] I published an earlier house built by Sunaryo in *The Asian House: Contemporary Houses of Southeast Asia*, Singapore: Select Books, 1993, pp. 30–5. Seventeen years later, by chance, I met the artist again at Selasar Sunaryo Art Space.
[2] I Bambang Sugiharto, *Sunaryo: Borderless Universe*, Bandung: Yayasan Selasar Sunaryo, 2007, p. 117.

Left A small shimmering blue lap pool is cut into the hillside.

Opposite below left The path to the entrance is a processional route traversing the hillside.

Opposite below right A contemplative guest reception space overlooks a *koi* pond.

Above right and right Framed views of the ever-changing landscape from the dining room and the guest reception area.

Below The lower terrace overlooks verdant agricultural land.

JAKARTA
ARCHITECT: BUDI PRADONO
BUDIPRADONO ARCHITECTS

azwar anas
house

Budi Pradono was born in Salatiga in 1970 and graduated from the Architecture Department of Duta Wacana Christian University, Yogyakarta, in 1995. He gained experience with practices in Sydney prior to establishing Budipradono Architects in 1999. In the same year, he took up the post of Visiting Lecturer at the University of Indonesia. From 2000 to 2002, he worked with Kengo Kuma & Associates in Tokyo before embarking on postgraduate studies in 2002–3 at the postgraduate laboratory of architecture at Berlage Institute in Rotterdam. Pradono describes his practice as "a research-based architectural firm that engages with changing lifestyles in the twenty-first century."[1]

At the time of the author's visit, Pradono had just returned from "Open City: Designing Coexistence," an International Architecture Biennale organized by the Netherlands Architecture Institute (NAI), where he had exhibited his research on the relationship between the gated settlement and the kampong and had examined the shift from a culture of "the street" to one of "the car and the mall." The architect is interested in ways of overcoming the inequalities in society and designing for coexistence by creating metaphorical "holes" in the walls surrounding gated settlements.

The Azwar Anas House is a 260-square meter residence with a complex program. The architect explains: "This is a contemporary urban house where the brief required that many programs had to be arranged in a relatively small space. A void is created at the center of the plan, with a one-meter space around the perimeter to maximize the amount of natural light entering the house." The parti for the design is essentially "a box within a box." Greenery is introduced on each level to reduce solar heat gain and in the interstitial space between the inner and outer boxes.

Explaining the design process, Pradono refers to the "programatic negotiation" that underlies the design development. "Internal spaces were required to be flexible so that the house can easily be reconfigured. The negotiation necessary in the program became the fundamental factor in the design evolution. Conflict between various requirements and interests had to be resolved and this was done with the use of glass sliding doors to separate functions or unify the

Pages 194–5 The house has a striking façade of pivoting timber louvers.

Left On axis with the entrance is a *koi* pond at the base of a deep lightwell.

Top The principal staircase is located at the perimeter of the ground floor.

Above Daylight casts an intriguing pattern on the stairs.

space. The sliding glass screens and solid walls are arranged around a central void that acts as a mediator. The void separates various space programs, yet permits them to be combined. The combined space can be used for family gatherings or communal prayers. The form and the façade treatment are the outcome of the programatic fragmentation."

A *feng shui* expert was commissioned to offer advice on the house orientation, the program and the processional route from the entrance. A large part of the ground floor is given over to a carport and garage, with a security post facing the street at the base of an external stair that gives access to a first-floor terrace. Other accommodations in the sub-basement include two bedrooms, a study, a *mushola* (prayer room) and *wudu* (ablution room). The entrance lobby is accessed from the first-floor terrace and is centrally located between the guest suite and a prayer room, the entrance door being concealed behind a "veil" in the form of a timber screen that extends the full width of the façade. Beyond the entrance lobby, and directly on axis, is a guest reception area.

A timber-floored deck leads to the central void, which has a reflecting pool flanked by the living area, the dining area and the dry kitchen. Conventionally, the driver's room, maidspace and kitchen are located at the rear of the house, accessed by a one-metre-wide staircase on the right flank of the house that bypasses the reception rooms.

From the living room, a concealed staircase ascends to the second floor, where some of the high-ceilinged bedrooms revive memories of a kampong dwelling with mattresses on raised platforms. From the second floor, a narrow circular staircase extends up to a roof garden. The plan and section of the house create an incredibly well-lit interior, with very good natural ventilation, but one that is simultaneously private and gives little indication of its openness when viewed from the street.

[1] Budi Pradono in conversation with the author, October 24, 2009.

Left The lightwell and the *koi* pond are the heart of the plan. Beyond is a glimpse of the spiral stair that gives access to the roof.

Above right, center and right There are numerous tactile details in the house.

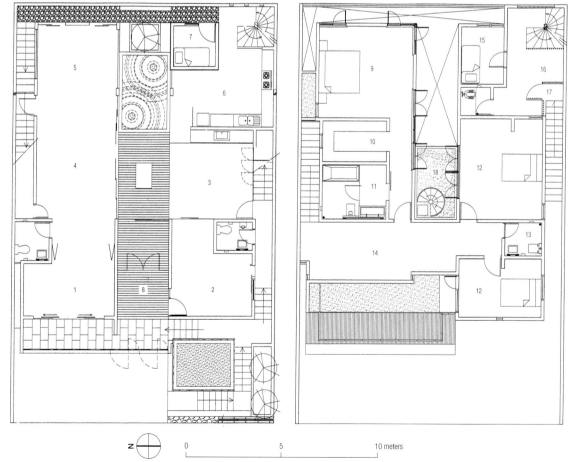

Key
1   Guest room
2   Prayer room
3   Dining room
4   Reading room
5   Living room
6   Kitchen
7   Maid's room
8   Entrance
9   Master bedroom
10 Dressing room
11 Master bathroom
12 Bedroom
13 Bathroom
14 Lobby
15 Driver's room
16 Drying area
17 Side entrance
18 Roof garden

N

0   5   10 meters

Left At rooftop level, there is a surprising garden terrace.

Above Section drawing.

Opposite below Ground and first floor plans.

Left, above center and above right Details of the pivoting timber screen fronting the first-floor veranda.

wisnu house

JAKARTA

ARCHITECTS: AHMAD & WENDY DJUHARA

DJUHARA + DJUHARA

Ahmad Djuhara was born in 1966 and graduated from Parahyangan Catholic University, Bandung, in 1991. He was first employed by Pacific Adhika Indonesia (PAI, 1992–8), later taking up an appointment with Jeffrey Budiman Architects (1999–2001). His designs have won a number of awards, including first place for the Megolopolis Gallery House, Tarumanagara University, Jakarta, in 1997, and an honorable mention in the JakArt@2000 Jakarta Arts Festival for an arts center selected by the sole American juror, architect Antoine Predock.

He established his own firm, Ahmad Djuhara, in 2001, and since 2004 has been in partnership with his wife Wendy in the firm djuhara + djuhara. Wendy Djuhara graduated three years after her husband from the same university and also worked with PAI, in her case for ten years. Their design for the Museum Wayang extension in Jakarta won first place in a competition organized by the Jakarta Chapter of the IAI and the Bureau for Culture and Museums in 2004. Both Ahmad and Wendy Djuhara are active members of Arsitek Muda Indonesia (AMI) and are occasionally referred to as the AMINext generation.

The Wisnu House is a modest town house shoehorned into a relatively tiny urban site at Perumahan Graha Indah in West Java. The site is approximately 5 m wide and 30 m deep, with a garden at right angles at the rear, the whole totaling 242 sq m. The house has a footprint of 5 m x 25 m and a built-up floor area of 215 sq m. Ahmad Djuhara explains that "The project was offered to djuhara + djuhara after Nugroho Sundari and Tri Sundari had seen the architects' earlier design for the low-budget Steel House at Bekasi. The clients were living on the site in a tiny 36-m terrace house on a 78-sq m plot. Piece by piece they bought the land behind their house, eventually acquiring a total of 242 sq m sloping down from the rear boundary. After buying the land, they had a limited budget to build the new house, which presented a challenge to the designers."[1]

The concept was to erect a "floating" box that shelters an open space at ground floor—a modern interpretation of the traditional *rumah panggung* (platform house). The ground floor is devoted to the living, dining and kitchen spaces, whereas the "box" above contains bedrooms, a sitting room overlooking a garden and a study. Wendy Djuhara explains that "the original idea of the floating box was influenced by cost considerations. The narrowness of the site allowed us to only build on the second level, while achieving an additional open living space below, perfect for living in the tropics."

The ground floor has a hinged steel metal gate at the front, with a smaller steel side gate, which functions as the main entrance to the house. The entire frontage can be opened up to connect the interior to the front garden and the public space across the street that contains a communal garden and sports facilities.

With the limited budget available, the basic structure of the house consists of concrete columns, beams and slab because, at the time of construction, a concrete structure was less expensive than a steel one. But the upper floor has a lightweight structure just 4 m wide consisting of a steel frame roofed with a metal deck. The main façade of the house, facing the street, is clad in reclaimed timber, intended to shield the interior from the western sun in the afternoon. The upper floor is accessed by a stair adjacent to the house

Pages 202–3 The low-budget house is shoehorned into a narrow urban site with amazing dexterity.

Above The house seen in its urban context.

Opposite The design is conceptually a floating box that opens up the ground-floor space,

entrance and also from the rear garden by an inclined steel bridge. Along the south flank of the building, a 600-mm gap has been left to permit sunlight to enter and also to allow rain to fall into a channel that directs water to the front of the site. The open-sided concept at ground-floor level permits cross-ventilation and allows the occupants to live without air-conditioning.

The house is designed for a family of two adults and two children and a live-in maid. Unusually, the servants' quarters are located at the front of the house, giving the domestic staff easy access, adequate sunlight and ventilation and responsibility for providing security for the house. This is a further development of the experimental design approach in the architects' earlier design for the Sugiharto Steel House. It brings the so-called back yard into use as the family recreation area, rejecting the notion that it is a back-of-house space for kitchens and domestic staff. Ahmad argues that the common perceptions of housing can be critically challenged through such design exploration.[2] Asked to reflect upon architects who have been influential in their careers, the Djuharas name Tom Elliott and the late Richard Dalrymple, both architects in PAI, together with Irianto Purnomo Hadi, the first "president" of AMI, in addition to Japanese contemporary architecture.

The house is designed with immense ingenuity, with overlapping functions and multiple levels. Ramps between floors follow the sloping topography and enable easy access. Like a "Matryoshka (Russian) doll," the house opens up to reveal numerous layers, with infinite possible variations of layout. Architect Danny Wicaksono observes that "Everyone who visits the house feels that this is a place that they could live in and they would feel comfortable in."[3] This a perceptive remark for, although of modest size, the house embodies the "original" idea of a "home," not least being the way its location and openness show faith in the enduring quality of community.

Ahmad accepts the opinion but responds: "I feel that this house is not a house for everybody. It takes some guts to live in such an extraordinary design in Jakarta or Indonesia, with open space at ground floor. It is even intimidating." More importantly, the house indicates how, with ingenuity, beautiful spaces can be created on a modest budget.

[1] Ahmad and Wendy Djuhara in conversation with the author, October 20, 2009.

[2] Amanda Achmadi, "Ahmad Djuhara: Steel House, Bekasi, Jakarta," in Geoffrey London (ed.), *Houses for the 21st Century*, Singapore: Periplus Editions, 2004, pp. 102–5.

[3] Danny Wicaksono in conversation with the author, October 18, 2009. Wicaksono is joint Editor-in-Chief of *Jong Arsitek*, a free architectural e-magazine based in Indonesia.

Left The kitchen/dining space looks out to a quiet rear garden.

Right There is considerable ingenuity in the overlapping of functions within the plan.

Below left The front façade of the house is clad in reclaimed timber.

Below right Light penetrates through the timber screen and casts a gentle filigree throughout the interior.

Top The concrete frame provides a memory of a former structure on the site.

Top right An inclined bridge leads from the garden to the first-floor family room.

Above and right The interior has multiple levels with connecting ramps.

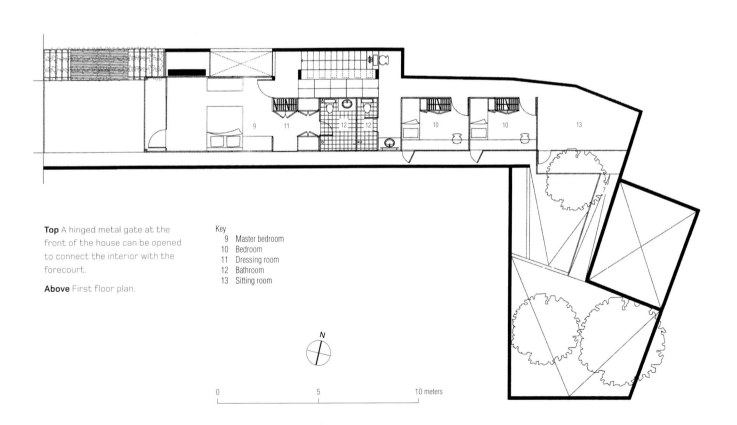

Top A hinged metal gate at the front of the house can be opened to connect the interior with the forecourt.

Above First floor plan.

Key
9   Master bedroom
10   Bedroom
11   Dressing room
12   Bathroom
13   Sitting room

N

0   5   10 meters

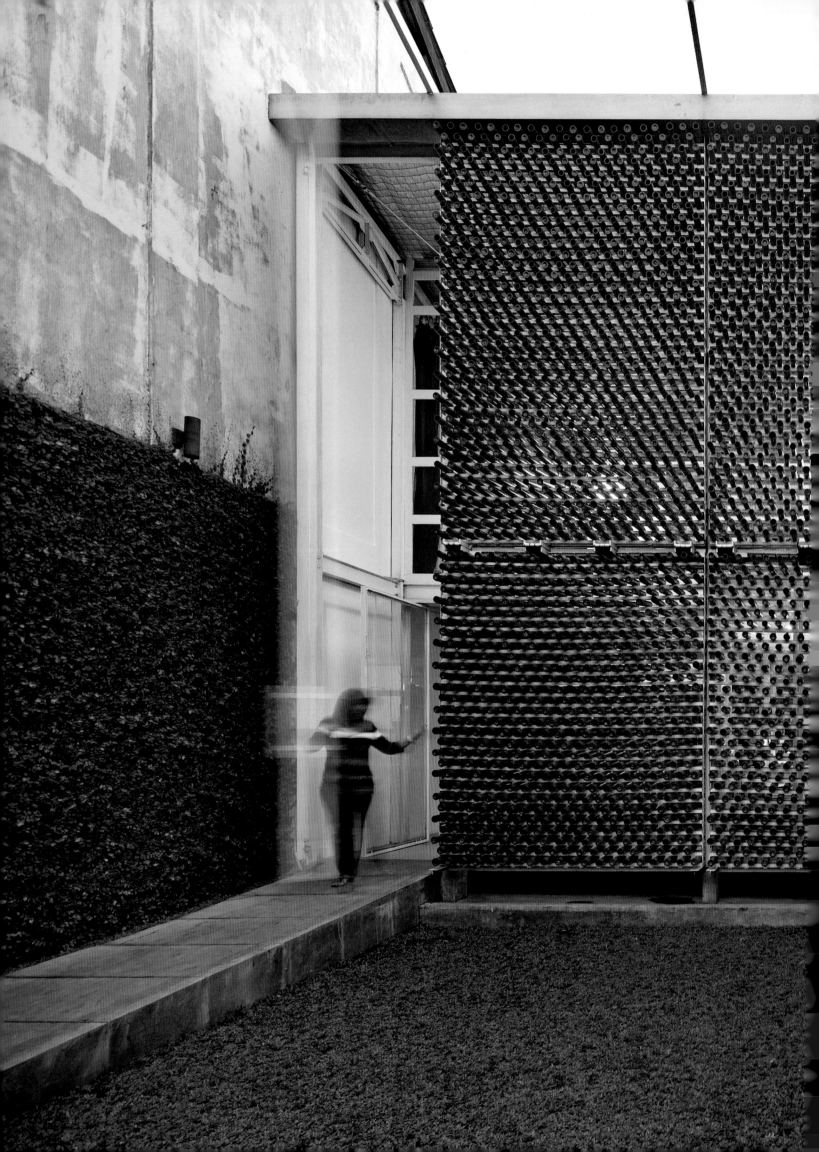

JAKARTA
ARCHITECT: BUDI PRADONO
BUDIPRADONO ARCHITECTS

ahmett salina
house and studio

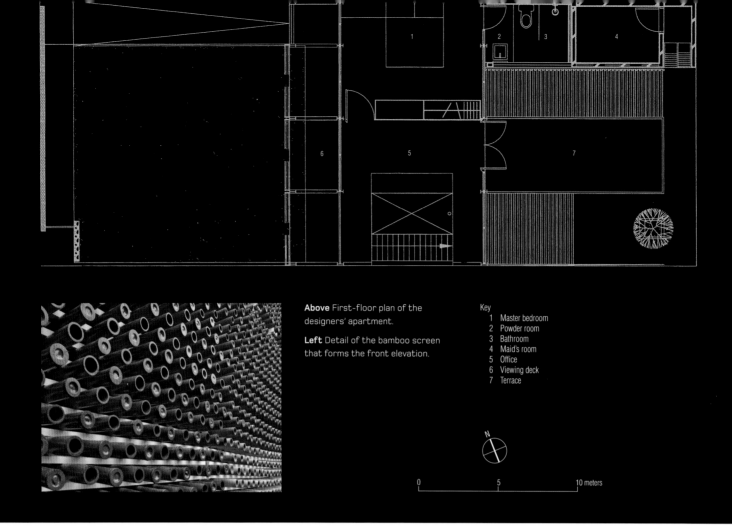

Above First-floor plan of the designers' apartment.

Left Detail of the bamboo screen that forms the front elevation.

Key
1 Master bedroom
2 Powder room
3 Bathroom
4 Maid's room
5 Office
6 Viewing deck
7 Terrace

0   5   10 meters

with all the paraphernalia of a modern office—a glass-topped work table, a cluster of Apple Macintosh computers, a designer bicycle, the ubiquitous water dispenser and a customer/client reception area—together with a neon sign bidding staff and visitors to "Change yourself." An open-riser staircase with cantilevered treads leads to the private zone, while the living and working spaces are visually connected by a void alongside the stair.

The living accommodation is basic; a mattress on the floor recalls memories of a kampong lifestyle. There is space in the small patio at the rear of the house for a table and four chairs—and a frangipani tree. A neighboring first-floor balcony overlooks the space, which harks back to the concept of community found in village culture. At the front of the house, the façade has been pushed back to create a grass forecourt. A pergola spans the low metal gate at the boundary, and a concrete ramp gently ascends to the entrance.

A modest replacement of a former terrace house in a neighborhood that was originally constructed as part of a 1960s Sukarno-era Russian-designed master plan, the home-office was built on a tight budget. The architect has used considerable ingenuity in sourcing appropriate

materials and in the elegant, if austere, detailing of the structure, the cladding and the internal finishes. A steel frame was employed for the house to speed up the construction process. The internal finishes are essentially unpainted plaster walls, polished cement and terrazzo floors, surface-mounted electrical conduit and exposed ducting, with, at first-floor level, an aluminum foil-insulated ceiling above exposed steel beams.

The house-cum-office is an appropriate base for one of Jakarta's trendiest young graphic design firms. There are parallels in the design approach of Budi Pradono with other practitioners in Southeast Asia, including Singaporean architect Ling Hao and Malaysian architect Kevin Low. Pradono is now working worldwide, and ongoing projects include the Pure Shin Si Lin exhibition space and the Flora Building project, both in Taipei, Taiwan. His work has also been published in several books and journals.[3]

[1] Budi Pradono in discussion with the author, October 25, 2009.

[2] Catherine Slessor, "Balinese Bamboo," *The Architectural Review*, December 2005, p. 84.

[3] Katharina Feuer, *Young Asian Architects*, Cologne: Daab Publishers, 2006.

Left A sign that is a product of the design company.

Right A narrow path leads to the house-studio entrance.

Below left A small patio at the rear of the house, with dining facilities for staff.

Below right A horizontally hinged bamboo screen forms the entrance façade.

puri indah house

JAKARTA
ARCHITECT: ADI PURNOMO
MAMOSTUDIO

Born in Yogyakarta in 1968, Adi "Mamo" Purnomo studied architecture at Gajah Mada University in Yogyakarta. He worked with Pacific Adhika Intermusa (PAI) in Jakarta and for a period in the 1990s with DP Architects in Singapore. He returned to Jakarta to set up his own architectural studio in 2000. By 2002 he had collected an Ikatan Arsitek Indonesia (IAI) Award for a series of three urban houses in Pamulang, Kebon Jeruk and Tomang that demonstrate affordable housing in both the suburban and kampong context. He represents a new generation of Indonesian architects. Mamostudio is deliberately kept small, "like a mosquito that touches the surface of water without being immersed in it. I am experimenting with the productivity of this kind of studio model," he says.[1] Purnomo is an active member of Arsitek Muda Indonesia (AMI), and he is now also an established critic and reviewer at several Indonesian universities. He has exhibited his work in Indonesia, the Netherlands and the USA.

The Puri Indah House is a stunning modern design for Dr Lau, a retired medical doctor turned painter/photographer, his wife Evie Miranda and their daughter Laura Stephanie. The three of them share an appreciation of art and are keen collectors so that the house is simultaneously a dwelling, an artist's studio and a private gallery that is occasionally open to the public. Their art collection includes the works of a number of Indonesian artists— Sudjana Kerton, Hendra Gunawan, Nasirun, Iwan Sagito, Agus Suwage, Entang W., Rudi Mantofani, Yunizar, Alfi, Yusra M., Irfan; as well as international artists Shu Xin Ping, Shen Xiao Tong, Shi Hu Stonetiger, Phillipo Scacia and Yuri Gorbachev— to name a few.

The house occupies a rectangular site opposite a supermarket, and like many town houses in Jakarta is literally turned inside out so that all the views are internalized, in this case forming a labyrinth of internal spaces dramatically lit by shafts of sunlight from above. At first, the complexity of the house plan and section is overpowering, with tilted walls and reflecting glass and water surfaces making it a challenge to comprehend the rationale of the plan and section. A sculptural figure, "Pasak Bumi" by Teguh Ostenrik, "climbing" an inclined wall, is reflected in the angled glass and appears to be suspended in space.

The materials used throughout are gray off-form concrete for the structure, unpainted gray plaster for the walls and smooth gray cement for the floors, which add to the cave-like ambience of the interior and heighten the impression of a subterranean space. The austere aura is augmented by music; at the time of the author's visit, a Gregorian chant echoed through the spaces. After a while, the logic of the geometry becomes apparent, and it becomes possible to navigate through the monochromatic landscape. The ability to orientate oneself is aided by the careful positioning and lighting of numerous paintings and sculptures. There are no significant views out from this house: it is designed to look inward, to be internalized and for the focus to be entirely on the works of art. All daylight comes from above, and areas of

Pages 216–17 The design is a sculptural composition employing concrete and light.

Above Sunlight slants into the living area.

Right The angular central atrium is a truly magical space.

Left Light falls upon a bridge within the atrium.

Right The play of light and shadow is mesmerising.

planting balance the somewhat austere sculptural interior. The house was designed some time after Adi Purnomo's pioneering book was published in 2005.

The book considered the rational reasons for design. Because the client of the Puri Indah house is a photographer and an art collector, light is an important element in the design. Purnomo thus posed the question: What possibilities are open when thinking about light in this context? What if the light becomes the material that creates the space? What if any preconceived ideas about form and space are eliminated? He therefore studied the characteristics of light for a whole year and how the light could penetrate the volume, by use of models. He allowed the observed phenomena, in this case, sunlight, to become the generator of the design.

The house was designed specifically with the idea that the sun would enter between 09.00 and 11.00 and again between 14.00 and 16.00. This has determined the sections of the house and the angle of inclination of the internal walls. The play of light and shadow creates a house of constantly changing internal patterns, in some places visually dynamic and in other areas restful and calm. Reflections are not accidental although some must have been surprising even to the architect.

The architect has explained it more fully: "This is an example of a period when I questioned whether rationality was hampering or promoting the creative process. Being a studio, gallery and house for a photographer and a painter, the space needs light to be the component that shapes the space. At first, I studied how the sun moves at latitude 06°11'5" S and longitude 106°44'2" E during a day and throughout the year on a site that will be enclosed with a 10 meter-high wall. When I started to extract the data and translate it into a diagram, I was able to read beauty in its form. Numbers and diagrams became a poetry that emerged from the prose of ration-

ality—the thing that I thought all this time was hampering the courage to spontaneously feel beauty. The whole structure is set up as a series of slanting walls, with the basic premise to catch and redistribute sunlight at certain hours of the day. The top floor is the gallery, receiving the most amount of light and least amount of humidity; the middle floor is for dwelling; and the ground floor is for public use. Circulation was placed in the sides, so that public access to the roof doesn't interrupt the privacy of the middle floors."[2]

The compound is accessed from a garage court. The complex internal geometry is not apparent from the entrance façade (another characteristic of Purnomo's architecture). The house is entered through a tall timber door whereupon the visitor encounters a shoulder-height concrete wall that partially blocks a direct axial view of the interior. To the right is a linear pond that penetrates alongside the party wall to the rear of the house, passing beneath the principal staircase, which is a straight flight attached to the party wall.

To the left on entering the house is a breakfast bar and kitchen, a somewhat unusual arrangement, for a kitchen is usually located at the rear of the house, out of sight of visitors. It appears to be a reference to the location of a kitchen in kampong houses. Immediately beyond the low wall is a sitting area beneath a central lightwell with a TV, again a curious arrangement. Further along, and on the same axis, is the principal dining space.

What is instantly apparent is the complex internal geometry, with bridges across lightwells, sharply angular structures and light lancing down from above, reflecting and refracting from sloping glass planes and placid horizontal water bodies. Strong tilted concrete planes are visible, yet the house is surprisingly intimate in its internal spaces. There is pure excitement engendered by the constantly shifting

perspectives as one moves through the house horizontally and vertically, and the joy of coming upon a startling painting or sculptural object integrated into the processional route. There are numerous highly original paintings and sculptures, some by the owner and others by several of Indonesia's best contemporary artists.

At the summit of the house is a roof garden with an orthogonal array of plant pots containing lemon grass that is said to discourage mosquitoes. The pots continue across the glass roof above the central lightwell, and this creates an amazing effect of a moving pattern on the walls when viewed from below—a kinetic work of art. The pots also cut out glare.

Asked to explain the influences on his work, Adi Purnomo admits to admiration of the work of Peter Zumthor and his concentration on material quality but the major influence on his architecture is, he says, "the daily things that affect our lives." Like the Malaysian architect Kevin Low, Adi Purnomo prefers to work alone or with one or, at most, two assistants.

To paraphrase Professor Abidin Kusno: "In the context of the Post-Suharto era, the works of Adi 'Mamo' Purnomo are distinctive if not representative of the new attitude of architects searching for alternative formal and spatial expressions.... Mamo takes up larger social issues even though this has never been explicitly stated as part of his design agenda ... through his architecture, Mamo seeks to constitute a culture of reconciliation for the city that has been deeply divided by the rich and the poor."[3]

This is an amazing house for it literally causes an involuntary intake of breath when entering. The house has an elusive quality—there is pleasure at every turn and surprise encounters with works of art at each significant juncture. The movement of the sun creates an ever-changing kaleidoscopic effect—the internal spatial quality is palpable.

In 2008, Purnomo was invited to be part of the ORDOS100-project in Mongolia, an opportunity he grasped to test his ideas in another context, and in the same year he was awarded the Gold Medal of the Ikatan Arsitek Indonesia.

[1] Adi Purnomo, *Relativitas: Arsitek di Ruang Angan dan Kenyataan* [Relativity: An Architect in Dream and Reality], Jakarta: Borneo Publications, 2005, p. 13.
[2] Adi Purnomo in conversation with the author, October 19, 2009.
[3] Abidin Kusno, "'Back to the City': Urban Architecture in the New Indonesia," in *The Appearances of Memory: Mnemonic Practices of Architecture and Urban Form in Indonesia*, Durham: Duke University Press, 2010, pp. 71–97.

Key
2 Living room
4 Guest bedroom
6 Water feature
11 Kitchen
16 Walk-in closet
17 Sitting area
21 Void
22 Storeroom
24 Gallery

Opposite above left Multiple images are reflected from glass balustrades.

Top Section through the lightwell.

Left, above center and right Sunlight penetrates into the interior and casts enchanting shadows on vertical and horizontal surfaces.

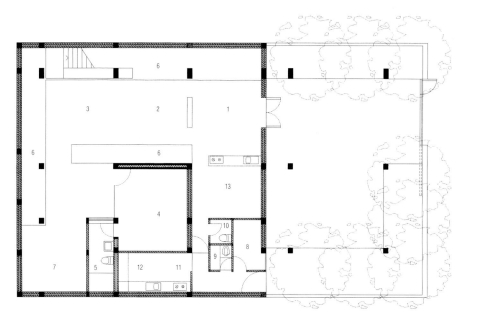

0   5   10 meters

Above Ground floor plan.

Below left A sculptural figure, Pasak Bumi, "climbs" an inclined wall.

Right Striking art works contrast sharply with cement-rendered walls.

Opposite above left An upper-level gallery space.

Opposite above right Plant pots containing lemon grass are located above the glazed roof and contribute a pattern of shifting shadows.

Opposite below The uncompromising entrance to the Puri Indah dwelling.

batanunggal mulia house

BANDUNG
ARCHITECTS: SUKENDRO SUKENDAR PRIYOSO & JEFFRY SANDY
NATANEKA ARSITEK

Sukendro Sukendar Priyoso was born in Jakarta in 1972 and is a graduate of Trisakti University, Jakarta. He went on to pursue graduate studies with the International Housing Study (IHS) group in Rotterdam. His partner, Jeffry Sandy, was born in 1975 and is also a graduate of Trisakti University. The two architects are members of the second generation of Arsitek Muda Indonesia, and having traveled to Japan with AMI on several occasions, the influence on their work of Tadao Ando and other Japanese architects is evident, particularly in their attention to detail and their use of daylight and texture. The two have also traveled to observe architecture, interior design and furniture in Milan, Barcelona and Granada, and have a shared interest in space planning acquired from their studies of the architecture of Louis Kahn.

Pages 226–7 The house is a meticulously detailed dwelling on the southern fringe of Bandung.

Above The water court is an extraordinarily calm space.

Opposite The entrance court is devoid of clutter.

The Batanunggal Mulia House is a modest link dwelling in a recently developed district of Bandung, off the southern bypass road. The individual houses in the street commonly have high walls, an internal courtyard, top light and a composed façade facing the public realm. Surrounded by generally anonymous architecture, the Batanunggal Mulia House is distinguished from it neighbors by the lucid articulation of its frontage.

The house is entered through a carport with a small garden to one side enclosed by a wall that affords some privacy. A permeable sliding door of steel mesh permits wind to flow through the house. Beyond the carport is a courtyard with a timber deck, a calm reflecting pool, a rectangular seat and a single tree. To the left on entering the house, via a pivoted timber door, is a raised timber platform that the architect describes as the equivalent of a *tatami* mat sitting space or *lesehan* in a Japanese house. Here, the owner has the option of sitting on a chair or on the floor in the manner found in a Sundanese restaurant or lying down with a book.

The essence of the house, however, is the manipulation of internal space and the precision of the detailing. The architects have evidently embraced the overlapping use of space in the traditional architecture of the Japanese *ryokan* or inn, where the multiple use of a relatively small floor area is achieved by exquisitely detailed storage that folds away into recesses. This is precisely what the architects have transferred to this dwelling, which exhibits an extraordinary minimalist quality and attention to tactile details utilizing a carefully selected palette of materials. There are no internal walls at ground level; rather, concealed cupboards and cabinets can be pulled out to form partitions or pushed into recesses to extend and order the interior space. The kitchen and maidspace are concealed at the rear of the house.

The manipulation of space is also evident in the way in which interior space is projected visually to embrace the courtyard so that a relatively small interior is made to appear much larger than it actually is. Reflective floor surfaces also extend the apparent size of the living area. The precise quality of detailing in smooth concrete, horizontal timber, steel mesh and toughened glass is best illustrated in the leading edge of the front façade that has an incredibly sharp arris.

The lasting impression of the house is its peaceful ambience. The unruffled surface of the pool in the courtyard and the uncluttered elegance of the interior create an atmosphere of extraordinary repose and calm.

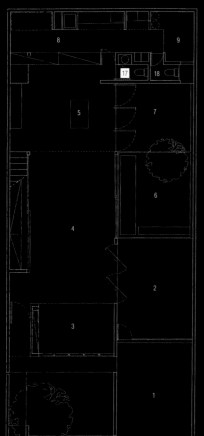

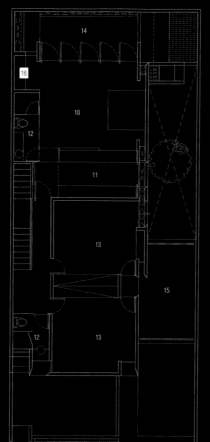

Key

1	Carport	10	Master bedroom
2	Garage	11	Wardrobe
3	Veranda	12	Bathroom
4	Living room	13	Bedroom
5	Dining room	14	Patio
6	Reflecting pool	15	Balcony
7	Pool deck	16	Workspace
8	Service area	17	Powder room
9	Drying area	18	Toilet

0   5   10 meters

Above The open-plan ground floor viewed from the dining area.

Left Ground and first floor plans.

Left, center and right : Details of the door to the patio, concealed shelves that slide out of a recess in the wall and a first-floor window overlooking the patio.

Below A minimalist approach is adopted in the design of the water court.

rumah
perbatasan

JAKARTA
ARCHITECT: YORI ANTAR
HAN AWAL & PARTNERS ARCHITECTS

Completed in 2009, Rumah Perbatasan is built on a typical rectangular urban housing plot in Jakarta, surrounded by high walls on three sides. Facing the street is an elegant sliding entrance gate with vertical platted metal slats. On entering the forecourt, the drive descends steeply to the basement garage, while to the left four steps lead to a timber deck where an intricately carved teak screen made by Ina Hansein directs visitors to the right, past a large painting on canvas depicting three dancing nudes by the Bali-born artist Putu Sutuwijaya, to a high breakfast bar at the very heart of the house. At this point, two steps lead down to the left to the main living area. The furniture includes a Corbusier-designed recliner and an armchair from the Kamu Collection. To the right, and behind a glazed screen, is the formal dining room. The route to the center of the house passes beneath a prominent sculpture by Alvin Titrowirjo located above the entrance.

Beyond the breakfast bar, which signifies the "pulse" of the dwelling, from which the whole ground floor is visible, are glazed sliding doors that open to a rear courtyard. The glass is shaded by the overhanging upper floor and by the tree canopy, but there is a sense of transparency and a continuum between the interior and exterior. When the doors are opened, air flows gently through the house and it is surprisingly cool without resorting to air-conditioning. The soothing sound of water descending a textured wall adds to the captivating ambience.

Behind the main staircase, and not immediately visible when entering the house, is the owner's study/home office, with a glass floor, which cantilevers over the swimming pool that runs parallel to the plot boundary. This "water court" is a magical space surrounded by tall mature trees designed in collaboration with the Bali-based landscape architect Karl Princic. The home office can also be accessed directly from the entrance to the house, thus bypassing the family rooms.

At first-floor level there is a family room, three bedrooms and a guest bedroom. Higher still, at rooftop level, is a gym/fitness room with a mirrored wall and exercise bar, a pool table, a piano area and a magnificent roof garden. A number of domestic staff maintain a discreet presence in accommodation provided behind the formal dining room.

The house can be enjoyed as a sensual experience. The gentle breeze flowing through the open doors, the sound of water splashing on stone, dappled sunlight and the music of a flute combine to soothe the spirit. The roof terrace is a cool escape from the city for evening entertainment. Art and architecture are indivisible in the house, with framed Venetian masks, a "Lolita" poster and a startling pink shower room integrated into the design.

The house has modernist lines with bold cantilevers softened by the rich texture of stone and timber that recalls memories of traditional architecture and interiors. It is the intention that the external walls, currently covered with a light steel mesh, will eventually be draped in vegetation that will connect with the rooftop terrace. In this way, Yori Antar gives modern Indonesian architecture a distinct identity.

Pages 232–3 An intimate bathing pool is located at the side of the house.

Above A short flight of stairs descends from the entrance to a garden court alongside the pool.

Left The shaded pool is surrounded by luxuriant vegetation.

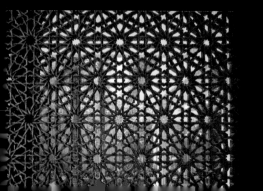

Left The living room opens out to a courtyard with a gentle fountain.

Below left First-floor plan and detail of entrance screen.

Above left and center Details of art works in the central stairwell.

Above right The study is a glazed box cantilevering over the pool.

Below The entrance façade is a coherent combination of tactile materials.

Select Bibliography

Achmadi, Amanda, "Indonesia: The Emergence of a New Architectural Consciousness of the Urban Middle Class," in Geoffrey London (ed.), *Houses for the 21st Century*, Singapore: Periplus Editions, 2004, pp. 28–35.

_____, "The Quest for a New Tropical Architecture," in Amir Sidharta (ed.), *25 Tropical Houses in Indonesia*, Singapore: Periplus Editions, 2006, pp. 8–18.

Akmal, Imelda, "The Architecture of 'Balinisation': An Investigation of Cultural Tourism Development in Bali," CSEAS Seminar Programme, Monash University, Melbourne, 2002.

_____, *Indonesian Architecture Now*, Jakarta: Borneo Publications, 2005.

Akmal, Imelda, Wendy Djuhara and P. Indrijati (ed.), *Karya-karya Arsitek Muda Indonesia 1997–2002/Works and Projects of Young Indonesian Architects 1997–2002*, Jakarta: Gramedia Pustaka Utama, 2002.

Al-Asad, Mohammad and Majd Musa (eds.), *Architectural Criticism and Journalism: Global Perspectives*, Turin: Umberto Allemandi for The Aga Khan Award for Architecture, 2006.

Budihardjo, Eko, *Architectural Conservation in Bali*, Yogyakarta: Gadjah Mada University Press, 1986.

Curtis, William J. R., *Modern Architecture Since 1900*, Oxford: Phaidon Press, 1982.

Feuer, Katharina, *Young Asian Architects*, Cologne: Daab Publishers, 2006.

Frampton, Kenneth, Gitta Domik, Elizabeth R. Jessup and John Cava (ed.), *Studies in Tectonic Culture: The Poetics of Construction in Nineteenth and Twentieth Century Architecture*, Chicago: MIT Press, 1995.

Goad, Philip and Anoma Pieris, *New Directions in Tropical Architecture*, Singapore: Periplus Editions, 2005.

Kusno, Abidin, "'Back to the City': Urban Architecture in the New Indonesia," in *The Appearances of Memory: Mnemonic Practices of Architecture and Urban Form in Indonesia*, Durham: Duke University Press, 2010, pp. 71–97.

Muynck, Bert de, "Regional Architecture Confronting with Indonesian Tropical Climate," in SPACE voice maker, ESpace, May 25, 2009.

Nalbantoglu, Gulsum Baydar and Wong Chong Thai (eds.), *Postcolonial Space(s)*, New York: Princeton Architectural Press, 1997.

Nas, Peter J. M. and Martien de Vletter (eds), *The Past in the Present: Architecture in Indonesia*, Rotterdam: NAi Publishers, 2007.

Noerzaman, Achmad et al, *Arkonin*, Jakarta: PT Arkonin, 2009.

Powell, Robert, *The Asian House: Contemporary Houses of Southeast Asia*, Singapore: Select Books, 1993.

_____, *The New Asian House*, Singapore: Select Publishing, 2001.

_____, *The New Malaysian House*, Singapore: Periplus Editions, 2008.

_____, *Singapore Houses*, Singapore, Tokyo and Vermont USA: Tuttle Publishing, 2009.

_____, *The Tropical Asian House*, Singapore: Select Books, 1996.

_____, *The Urban Asian House: Living in Tropical Cities*, Singapore: Select Books, 1998.

Powell, Robert (ed.), *Architecture and Identity: Exploring Architecture in Islamic Cultures 1*, Singapore: Concept Media for The Aga Khan Award for Architecture, 1983.

_____, *The Architecture of Housing: Exploring Architecture in Islamic Cultures 4*, Geneva: The Aga Khan Award for Architecture, 1990.

_____, *Regionalism in Architecture: Exploring Architecture in Islamic Cultures 2*, Singapore: Concept Media for The Aga Khan Award for Architecture, 1987.

_____, *Regionalism: Forging an Identity*, Singapore: School of Architecture, National University of Singapore, 1991.

Prawato, Eko Agus, *2 x 50 = 100*, Yogyakarta: Duta Wacana University Press, 2009.

Ricouer, Paul, "Universal Civilisations and National Cultures," in Charles A. Kelbley (trans.), *History and Truth*, Evanston: Northwestern University Press, 1965, pp. 271–84.

Sidharta, Amir (ed.), *25 Tropical Houses in Indonesia*, Singapore: Periplus Editions, 2006.

Sutanto, Sonny, "AMI 2002," in Imelda Akmal, Wendy Djuhara and P. Indrijati (ed.), *Karya-karya Arsitek Muda Indonesia 1997–2002/ Works and Projects of Young Indonesian Architects 1997–2002*, Jakarta: Gramedia Pustaka Utama, 2002, pp. 20–1.

Tjahjono, Gunawan, "Young Indonesian Architects: The Exploration 1990–1995," in Imelda Akmal, Wendy Djuhara and P. Indrijati (ed.), *Karya-karya Arsitek Muda Indonesia 1997–2002/Works and Projects of Young Indonesian Architects 1997–2002*, Jakarta: Gramedia Pustaka Utama, 2002, pp. 26–9.

Magazines and Journals

Architectural Review, No. 1306, London, December 2005.

A+U, No. 12, Tokyo, 2005.

Space, Singapore, April/May 2000.

Directory of Architects

Adi Purnomo
mamostudio
Jl. Taman Tangkuban Prahu 20
Jakarta, Indonesia
+62 813 85379406
www.mamostudio.com

Ahmad and Wendy Djuhara
djuhara + djuhara
Jl. Galunggung 764—Ciputat
Tangerang 15414, Indonesia
+62 813 11287521/816 726908
djuhara@djuhara.com

Andra Matin
andramatin
Jl. Manyar III Blok 03 Kav 30 No. 4-6
Sektor 1 Bintara Jaya
Jakarta 12330, Indonesia
+62 21 7353338/73692258
andra168@cbn.net.id

Antony Liu and Ferry Ridwan Architects
PT Dwitunggal Mandirijaya
Ruko Puri Kencana Niaga D1-3J
Jl. Aries Utama
Jakarta 11620, Indonesia
+62 21 5857994/58904897
dwitunggalmandiri@yahoo.com

Budi Pradono
Budipradono Architects
Jl. Walet 6 Blok 1.2 No. 11
Sektor 2 Bintaro Jaya
Jakarta 12330, Indonesia
+62 21 7370367
www.budipradono.com

Chan Soo Khian
SCDA Architects Pte Ltd
8 Teck Lim Road
Singapore 088385
+65 6324 5458
www.scdaarchitects.com

Denny Gondojatmiko
Denny Gondo Architect
Jl. S Citarum h17, Sec V
BSD City, Tangerang
Jakarta 15322, Indonesia
+62 21 5315 3773
www.studioairputih.com

Eko Agus Prawoto
Eko Prawoto Architecture Workshop
Jl. Bener Gang Pandanwangi No. 11
Yogyakarta 55243, Indonesia
+62 274 622324
ekoprawoto@yahoo.com

Gregorius Supie Yolodi
and Maria Rosantina
d–associates
Jl. Bangka 8C No. 23.
Jakarta 12720, Indonesia
+62 21 7183214
www.d-associates.com

Kusuma Agustianto
Kusuma Agustianto Architecture Studio
Kemang Point Buildings 2nd Floor (2-05B)
Kemang Raya 3, Jakarta 12730, Indonesia
+62 217 193660
www.kusumaagustianto.com

M. Ridwan Kamil
Urbane Architects
Sumur Bandung 20
Bandung 40132, Indonesia
+62 22 2500453
www.urbane.co.id

Popo Danes
Popo Danes Architect
Jl. Hayam Wuruk 159
Denpasar 80235
Bali, Indonesia
+62 361 242659
www.popodanes.com

René Tan and Quek Tse Kwang
RT+Q Architects
32A Mosque Street
Singapore 059510
+65 6221 1366
www.rtnq.com

Sekar Warni
Uttara Indonesia
Jl. Drupadi 88A, Basangkasa
Seminyak, Bali 803361, Indonesia
+62 361 733799/736400
nawa_9@indo.net.id

Sukendro Sukendar Priyoso and
Jeffry Sandy
nataneka arsitek
Jl. Panglima Polim 8 No. 2 Pav
Jakarta 12160, Indonesia
+62 21 70118770
kendro.sp@gmail.com

Sunaryo
Selasar Sunaryo Art Space
Jl. Bukit Pakar Timur, Bandung
Indonesia
sunaryo@gmail.com

Tan Tik Lam
Tan Tik Lam Architects
Jl. Gempol Wetan 113
Bandung 40115
West Java, Indonesia
+62 22 4209476
ttla_bdg@yahoo.com

Tan Tjiang Ay
Jl. Jati Murni 33B
Jati Padang-Pasar Minggu
Jakarta 12540, Indonesia
+62 21 7891808
tantjiangay@yahoo.com

Walter Wagner
Habitat 5
Jl. Goa Gong, Banjar Santi Karya,
Ungasan, Kuta Selatan Bali 80362
+62 361 8481755
habitat5@indosat.net.id or
habitat@habitat5.com
www.habitat5.com

Yoka Sara
Bale Legend Architect
Jl. Durian 16, Denpasar 80232
Bali, Indonesia
+62 361 249244
www.yokasara.com

Yori Antar
Han Awal & Partners Architects
Jl Palem Puri No. 7
RT 003/RW 06
Serua Poncol—Sawah Baru
Bintaro Jaya Sektor IX
Tangerang 15413, Indonesia
+62 21 7457797/7454397
www.yoriantar.com

Architect and Writer
Robert Powell
R5 Marine Gate, Marine Drive
Brighton BN2 5TN, UK
+44 (0) 1273 624855
robertpowell42@yahoo.co.uk

Photographer
Albert Lim KS
12 Koon Seng Road,
Singapore 426962
+65 96425350
albertlim55@yahoo.com.sg

Acknowledgments

My first experience of the warmth and hospitality of the people of Indonesia was in 1979 as one of a group of environmental planners and scientists who were tasked by the Indonesian Institute of Sciences (LIPI) with surveying and recording the flora and fauna of a proposed nature reserve at Morowali in Central Sulawesi. At that time, I was an architect and master planner in practice in the UK. Accessing this remote 200,000-ha area in the rain forest was a logistical challenge—via a scheduled flight from Jakarta to Ujung Pandang and then by twin-propeller light aircraft to a grass strip at Kendari; thereafter by Pelni Line steamer up the east coast of Sulawesi to Kolonodale, and finally across the Gulf of Teluk Tolo to Morowali on the Ranu River by fishing *perahu* (a boat with outriggers carved from a single large tree). I lived for five months in the rain forest alongside the native Wana people and with coastal Bugis fishermen and encountered the remote indigenous Kayu Merangka tribe. I slept in a primitive hut in the Uewaja Valley, and in March 1980 I contributed a draft Management Plan for the Morowali National Park.[1]

Four years later, in 1984, I joined the staff of the National University of Singapore as Associate Professor of Architecture, and during my first vacation I set out on another journey, first to Bogor and the Botanic Gardens at Cibodas and then to Yogyakarta via the Puncak Pass to visit the Sultan's Kraton, and onwards to Borobudur, Prambanan and the Plain of Kings. I ascended Gunung Bromo on horseback and made my way by ferryboat to Gilimanuk on the north coast of Bali where I boarded a local bus to Singaraja, and finally to Ubud and Kuta. This then was my introduction to the Indonesian archipelago.

In writing this book, I have to thank a number of architects who helped me to source the most innovative new houses in Indonesia. They include Kusuma Agustianto, Yori Antar, Ernesto Bedmar, Jeffrey Budiman, Chan Soo Khian, Popo Danes, Ahmad and Wendy Djuhara, Denny Gondo, Cosmas D. Gozali, Irianto Purnomo Hadi, Ridwan Kamil, Willis Kusuma, Antony Liu, Andra Matin, Glenn W. Parker, Budi Pradono, Eko Agus Prawoto, Adi "Mamo" Purnomo, Ferry Ridwan, Jonathan Quek, Patrick Rendradjaja, Jeffry Sandy, Sardjono Sani, Yoka Sara, Sukendro Sukendar Priyoso, René Tan, Tan Tik "Lemy" Lam, Tan Tjiang Ay, Baskoro Tedja, Walter Wagner, Judistira Wananda, Sekar Warni and Gregorius Supie Yolodi.

On behalf of Albert Lim KS and myself, I wish to thank the owners of the houses who permitted us to photograph their homes, including Azwar Anas, Irwan Ahmett and Tita Salina, Mr and Mrs Karta Laksana Kamarga, Eric Chang and Catherine Widjaja, Karadi Hanan, Anton and Juliewati Hudyana, Winfred Hutabarat, Thierry and Clo Joulin, Kang Kie Liong and Peggy, Ati Ibu Kie Soei Lan, Dr Lau and Evie Miranda, Mr and Mrs Radius Muntu, Joelianto Noegroho, Ryan and Teresa Padget, Karl and Dhea Princic, Mulyo Rahardjo, Iwan and Windy Rialdy,

Christophe Rougeron, Saksono Banyuaji, Sitok Srengenge and Farah Maulida, Sugihati, Sunaryo, Michael Tan, and Nugroho Wisnu and Sundari. Other owners wished to remain anonymous.

My thanks go also to numerous individuals who entertained us, advised us or helped us on our way to sometimes remote destinations, among them Anton Clark of Prestige Bali Villas, Shinta Devi, Pak Edo, Elias Hariwordo, Maryati B. Imanto, Kadek Karnawa, Grace Kartono, Eku Lamu, Eka Lanus, Hendyanto Lim, Patrick Lim, Irra Malik of Alila Soori, Ketut Midana, Nugroho, Titus Nurabadi, Jean-Marie Peloni and Domonique Seguin, Fransiska Prihado, Mulyo Rahardjo, Meta Rahmani, Saksu, Indra Santoso K., Putu Edy Semara, Tony Sofian, Yandi Prayudhi, Yanto Widodo, Kompyang Widyastuti, Made Wijaya, Budi S. Wita and Yu Sing.

Special thanks also go to Tan Tjiang Ay and Tan Tik Lam for their hospitality in Bandung and to Danny Wicaksono of mamo-studio for generously acting as our guide in Jakarta.

Eric Oey and the staff of the Periplus Publishing Group, and Judi Suwidji, Yohana and Didik of Java Books Indonesia, were also immensely helpful in identifying houses to include in the book and coordinating our travel. I thank too our patient and resourceful drivers, Pak Amal in Jakarta and Wayan Subrato in Bali. Thanks also to Noor Azlina Yunus for her meticulous editing of my text.

Belated thanks go also to architect Gordon Benton, now with Lippo Karawaci, who welcomed me to Indonesia in 1979; to Suha Özkan who, as Deputy Secretary-General of the Aga Khan Award for Architecture, kickstarted my career as a writer in 1985; to Lena Lim U Wen and William Lim SW, who published my first book on the design of contemporary Southeast Asian dwellings in 1993 and essentially created a market for the genre; to Lynda Lim Kwee Guek, my eyes and ears in Singapore, and to Albert Lim Koon Seng and Linda Lim with whom I have collaborated for twenty years. Albert's brilliant photographs surpass the work of any of his contemporaries in Asia.

And, finally, thanks to my wife Shantheni Chornalingam and our daughter Zara Shakira for their continued support in this passion I have for the architecture of Southeast Asia.

[1] See www.morowalinationalpark.com. The work on the Morowali National Park was assisted by Scottish architect Gordon Benton, later to become Senior Executive of Lippo Karawaci and the creative force behind Lippo Village.